SOCIALISM
AND WAR

EDVARD KARDELJ

Socialism and War

A SURVEY OF CHINESE CRITICISM
OF THE POLICY OF COEXISTENCE

Translated from the Serbo-Croatian by
ALEC BROWN

McGRAW-HILL BOOK COMPANY, INC.

New York

Printed in Yugoslavia
by "Jugoslavija" Publishing House

CONTENTS

Introduction

For a considerable time the columns of the Chinese press and the speeches of many official Chinese spokesmen — including even the highest state and party leaders—have been full of all sorts of attacks on Yugoslavia's foreign policy, and particularly on our concepts regarding the peaceful, active coexistence of states with differing social systems.

I say attacks because this is obviously not a case of normal criticism, least of all of a form of criticism within the socialist movement, but of a definite, hostile political campaign, conducted and organized with unusual passion and obviously with the intention that the campaign should exert a definite political pressure not only on Yugoslavia and Yugoslav communists, but also on much broader areas of the political developments of our time. Indeed, the very passion with which the campaign is conducted shows that here something much more important is involved than Chinese dissatisfaction with Yugoslav foreign policy, that is, with the policy of one of the smaller countries of Europe, which—even if it committed the most serious errors—could not in any way constitute a threat to China or damage Chinese socialism. It is obvious that the pressure of these Chinese attacks is directed against the entire front of the international policy of present-day socialism with the aim of extorting certain precise solutions of the dilemmas which face the forces of socialism in the present-day world. Today it is clear to everyone that the Chinese attacks are not aimed solely or primarily at Yugoslavia, but at any socialist forces whatsoever which fail completely to endorse the assumptions of China's foreign policy regarding these dilemmas.

Of the epoch-making significance of the Chinese revolution we are of course well aware. For this reason we have no intention whatsoever of examining all the aspects of that revolution exclusively through the prism of the Chinese-Yugoslav differences of opinion of the moment. Therefore, if we do criticize certain aspects of Chinese policy, this does not at all mean that we lose sight of the good that the Chinese revolution has done, and is still doing, in the world of today. We are also aware that the victory of the Chinese revolution was the work of the internal revolutionary forces of China which—under the leadership of the Communist Party—won through to this victory against an exceptionally powerful alliance of imperialism and Chinese reactionaries. The victory won under such circumstances created a whole series of capable revolutionary cadres in China, and in the ranks of the Chinese revolution and Communist Party most vigorously developed both a feeling of self-reliance and an awareness of the indispensability of working out and deciding the paths of that revolution independently. All these are unquestionably factors both very satisfactory and creative so long as the revolution faces inwards, concerned with its own development and advancement. However, they turn into something quite the opposite, that is, into a definite form of would-be domination of others, the moment the same revolution attempts either by force or by political pressure to impose itself and its way of looking at concrete problems on others. Therefore, when we criticize certain aspects of Chinese policy, particularly those connected with

Chinese attacks on socialist Yugoslavia, we have no intention of offering the communists of China our ideological views in exchange for theirs, but merely wish to prevent the imposing of alien patterns on ourselves. That is, in principle we reject a would-be domination hiding behind the watchword of a revolution, just as we reject the domination which the remnants of present-day imperialism would like to impose on us.

In the analysis of the development of the revolution, Yugoslav communists have never been governed by personal motives, but have always striven to base their analysis of this too on the scientific, Marxist method. The revolution in one country and the revolution in another are not one and the same thing. The extent to which in a given revolution socialist factors and relationships find expression, are maintained and develop, and the extent to which other social factors—such as the vestiges of the bourgeoisie, the property-owning mentality, general economic backwardness, bureaucracy, *étatism*, great-power chauvinism, nationalism, and so forth—impose their influence, is dependent on many internal social factors and material conditions. It is not a rare occurrence for revolutionary slogans to remain while the substance has been changed. When making an objective analysis one should try to separate what is subjective from what is objective, that is, not allow slogans or political declarations to conceal insight into the real substance of things.

In a Marxist analysis China is not merely the abstract conception of a socialist country. Socialism, too, is a reality. Socialism is a process in which extremely varied groupings of quantitative, and thereby also qualitative, relations find expression. In other words, behind the same ideological patterns there may be "much" or "little" socialism, "many" or "few" non-socialist factors and elements. These differences cannot be overcome by any wishful prescriptions about unity, for they are dependent on the actual social-economic set-up and on the nature of the personal factors which, even if they bear the same names, also differ, particularly when they become the ruling force. It would therefore be equally wrong to "deny" the socialist character of a country, if we do not happen to agree with it in our views regarding this or that problem of the moment, just as it would be wrong to think that the mere fact that a country is on the socialist road automatically means the end of any possibility of a divergence of views, even of sharply opposed views. So long as powerful factors of the old order and of state-administrative methods affect the development of socialism, such sharp oppositions of outlook are always a possibility. They are no longer unavoidable, but they are possible, particularly if what is obsolete and conservative tries to impose itself on other countries by force, in the name of socialist solidarity and of socialist ideology. Precisely for this reason any tendency of wanting to dominate others is in profound opposition to the elementary interests of world socialism.

The development of the Chinese revolution has lately entered a new phase, in which all the material and social factors of Chinese society exert their influence to the full, giving this development a specific path and form. Further, that internal development also has its international political expression. We, of course, have no wish to interfere in China's internal development, but since the international political repercussions of this directly affect both us and international socialism, we must get a clear picture of the sources and the real essence of the conceptions underlying current Chinese international policy, a constituent part of which is the Chinese anti-Yugoslav campaign.

The Yugoslav communists have to the very utmost avoided engaging in polemics, giving only the most essential answers to attacks, for the simple reason that they have always considered that it is precisely when differences of opinion actually exist that one should make every effort to bring out whatever may unite rather than what divides.

Between ourselves and the leadership of the Communist Party of China there are indeed differences of opinion regarding various aspects of the building of socialism and the elaboration of a socialist international policy. But there are still more interests which are common, before all others the factor of socialist solidarity, to which the leading communists of China so often refer. Under these circumstances it would be normal to promote intensive cooperation in those fields where these common interests are obvious and undisputable and leave it to further practice, to the development of socialist thought and to democratic socialist discussion to create the conditions for the settlement of differences of opinion, all the more so since, if one's real concern is the basic interest of socialism, differences of opinion are not only not harmful, but are the law of progress, the only possible form of the contest of ideas.

Those who formulate Chinese policy are clearly of a different opinion. They want subordination and not a democratic resolution of differences of opinion. For this reason they stubbornly continue their unprincipled campaign, in which their criticism of Yugoslav foreign policy is obviously only a tactical aim, which has a far vaster "strategic aim" behind it, namely, that of subordinating the entire policy of international socialism to their own conceptions or rather to the interests upon which those conceptions are based.

We however have no intention of being such an object, and we cannot allow anybody in the name of "true Marxism" to distort the sense of Yugoslav policy to suit their own requirements, that is, in order to conceal the real sense of their own policy, without giving them an answer. The Yugoslav people have the right to know the real reasons for the Chinese campaign against socialist Yugoslavia. Besides, it concerns not merely Yugoslavia, but also a much vaster complex of problems of present-day socialism. Precisely for this reason it is necessary to examine the deeper import and the ultimate consequences of the Chinese attacks on Yugoslav foreign policy, and look into the role and historical purpose of the political trend which finds expression in these attacks.

It is my desire with this treatise to make a contribution to the examination of these questions. I do not, of course, intend to deal with the slanders, insults and falsehoods, which prove nothing, but merely throw light on a pragmatic political ethic by which those who develop it show the world that in their country the true spirit of socialism is at a very low stage of development, while a sense of monopolistic supremacy lords it grandly. The authors of the anti-Yugoslav slander campaign obviously consider that sheer might plus formalistic references to socialist ideology permit them to go to the limits of unscrupulousness in their attempts to advance their own political conceptions and interests. However, the subject of analysis of the present study should be not so much the attacks on Yugoslav foreign policy in themselves

12

as the inner substance of the political ideology which produces such attacks. Therefore, the purpose of this explanation of the Chinese anti-Yugoslav campaign is in the first place to answer two questions: first, do the Chinese conceptions of international policy, which underlie this campaign, really derive from socialism and Marxism, as the authors of this policy maintain and, secondly, what is the actual historical effect of those conceptions, that is to say, what are they in actual fact and where do they lead, no matter what their authors make them out to be, or what they may actually believe they are.

CHAPTER 1

Chinese Ideology and Chinese Reality

If from a mass of empty words, slanders, verbalist dialectics and general political slogans we extract the real substance of the Chinese charges against Yugoslav foreign policy, they boil down to the following basic arguments.

The first argument is that the Yugoslav communists are revisionists and their revisionism derives from their fear of imperialism and war. This cowardice of theirs has persuaded them to pursue an opportunist policy of compromise with the bourgeoisie and with imperialism. Thereby they have sunk from the position of a revolutionary settlement of accounts with capitalism to that of reformism and now accept the theory of the peaceful growing of capitalism into socialism. To conceal this, the Yugoslav communists embellish imperialism. Consequently, they assist American imperialism. To that end they have even invented the policy of active coexistence, which is nothing less than a device for the concealment of their opportunist policy.

The second argument says that in contradistinction to this Yugoslav "opportunism" Chinese communists are not afraid either of imperialism or of war. They are for a radical settlement of accounts between the world of socialism and that of imperialism in a revolutionary clash. If this turns into war, it will be a just war and one should not be afraid of it or renounce it, because the sacrifices will soon be recompensed.

Further, the Chinese communists say that the assertion of the possibility of any lasting coexistence between the world of socialism and the world of capitalism and imperialism is illusory and harmful.

They consider that sooner or later a conflict between these two worlds is inevitable. As these Chinese theorists see it, there can be talk of coexistence, disarmament, the policy of agreement, and so forth, solely for the purpose of unmasking imperialism. On the other hand, to take the principle of coexistence to be a lasting and essential principle of socialist international policy would according to these conceptions be tantamount to renouncing the revolutionary method of resolution of the social contradictions of the present-day world. To speak today about peaceful means of struggle for the transition from capitalism to socialism, that is, to the rule of the working-class is, according to those conceptions, not only unrealistic—as by rule cannot the proletariat overcome counter-revolutionary violence otherwise than by revolutionary violence—but also senseless and opportunistic, for at a time when the strength of the socialist countries is growing so rapidly, these countries should not renounce the possibility of settling accounts with imperialism in a revolutionary way, and should not run away even from war.

If we reduce these arguments to what is fundamental—as seen through Chinese spectacles—we get the following picture: the Yugoslav communists are opportunists, whereas the Chinese communists are radical revolutionaries. It goes without saying that both these contentions are proved from the point of view of "genuine Marxism"—from a pedestal, so to speak, of infallibility—and so quotations are made to fit and the classics of Marxism are interpreted arbitrarily. In fact, both arguments are equally false: their aim is equally to distort the true picture of things and to cloud the real essence of the difference of opinion.

At the very first glance it is clear this picture reflects a highly simplified and sectarian understanding of the Marxist postulates about the socialist revolution. Further, it is obvious that in some cases these "genuine Marxists" of China have only been concerned to bother about Marxism to the extent necessary for the successful application of a familiar and indeed notorious method of unprincipled struggle. For the trick based on the calculation that the easiest way of discrediting and stifling a progressive idea is to make it out to be its own opposite, is old and well known. However, in the application of such methods, the Chinese theorists clearly forget that with the present-day wide extension of socialism and socialistic forces these methods are becoming increasingly worthless. Today socialist thought has become the substance of the conscious social action of such a huge number of people and so many nations throughout the world that whether they like it or not the age of the "great source of wisdom", Stalin, with his monopoly of holding out a truth which nobody dared gainsay, has passed, and with it the age of any great personality cult. It will only harm the Chinese communists themselves if they take over this compromised legacy of the past.

Let us now, in contradistinction to this cooked-up piece of Chinese "ideology", glance at the facts and make an attempt to elucidate the real essence of the differences of opinion on matters of socialist international policy, not excluding either the question of the so-called peaceful transition to socialism, which for quite definite reasons the Chinese theoreticians—and not we—tie up with those differences of opinion.

Here the first thing we have to do is to draw attention to the fact that the authors of these Chinese attacks on our policy make great efforts to lend those attacks the appearance of ideological and theoretical differences of opinion about Marxism. This is a device as hypocritical as it is anti-Marxist. By it, in fact, the Chinese critics of Yugoslavia are—both deliberately and unwittingly—striving to conceal the real, material essence of the matter.

Of course, there are ideological differences of opinion. We have our own opinion of the "Marxism" of the Chinese authors who are attacking Yugoslavia, though without considering ourselves immune to criticism of the sole "genuine" interpreters of Marxism. But the essence of the matter is not to be explained by ideological differences of opinion alone.

In the history of humanity so far, ideological differences have more often than not assumed one of two aspects. Either they were barren scholastic wrangles in the sphere of religious-dogmatic abstractions and a very narrow circle of people, or they were the outward reflection of real political and economic-social contradictions. In the development of modern socialist thought we meet with both sorts of ideological differences of opinion, but in the case of the Chinese attacks on Yugoslavia we clearly have to do in the main with the second sort.

In all this the sterile attempts of the Chinese authors to force Marxism on to a pragmatic ideological last, shaped to suit certain political needs, do not make any difference, since in the last resort, to repeat an often quoted saying of

18

Marx's, "people are not what they believe themselves to be, but what they really are". For this applies to the communists as much as it does to any other conscious being on this globe. However much the Chinese communists try to wrap themselves in the robes of defenders of "genuine" Marxism, their ideology is eloquent of their own social reality and its problems. And for those problems we certainly have a much greater understanding than we have for the "Marxism" which these Chinese essayists have reduced to the level of a coolie forced to bear all the burden of a disgusting political campaign against socialist Yugoslavia. In other words, for us it is simply a question of what, taken historically, in this Chinese campaign against our foreign policy and against the principle of coexistence really means. How to analyse this problem we are shown by precisely that Marxism which the Chinese article-writers so mercilessly exploit for their day-to-day practical needs.

Of course, I have not the slightest intention of discussing whose "Marxism" is the better or "more correct", the "Yugoslav" or the "Chinese"—or any other Marxism. Like every science Marxism is accessible to all, but the extent to which anyone has applied that science in practice is something not dependent merely on his desire to be a Marxist. This is why we do not reproach the Chinese critics for the fact that their Marxism merely serves to conceal their policy—which happens to be just what they reproach us with. But neither is it our view that anybody's policy or any sort of policy can be justified by quotations from the classics of Marxism and Leninism or monopolistically imposed as the "sole Marxist" policy, for a subjectivist self-justification of that sort, even if sincere, never has more than a relative value.

As is frequently emphasized, Marxism is not a dogma but a guide to action. Consequently *to appraise anybody's work, what is decisive is not the extent to which he has found fitting quotations to justify this or that act or his personal view of the Marxist guide, but what the actual social-historical effect of that work is.* Only that effect shows whether anyone has made good or bad use of the guide.

Besides, today so many and such diverse social factors speak up in the name of Marxism that it is obviously senseless for anyone to pretend to be the only "true" protagonist of a "true" Marxism. Marxism has furnished a series of scientific discoveries in the field of social development and together with these has evolved an epoch-making scientific method for the analysis of social contradictions, that is to say, for a more conscious steering of social developments than had ever been possible in the past. In this way Marxism has influenced, and indeed continues to influence, the whole "range" of social consciousness, from people who deny it in general to those who say they are the only "true" Marxists. Why, even the bourgeois political economy of our time has acquired what is genuinely new and scientific in it mainly from Marxism, however much it may deny this. It is precisely in this wide range of the influences it has exercised and still exercises on the social developments of our day that the epoch-making significance of Marxism as a science resides.

Thus, although Marxism is an indispensable weapon for any conscious and progressive socialist action, nevertheless, on the other hand, the mere formal acceptance of Marxism, or some aspects of Marxism, does not automatically make anyone either the most progressive or an infallible social force. In socialist conditions too men's minds and their actions are the resultant of the interlocking of extremely varied factors and processes: material developments, mental reactions, individual characteristics, traditions, manifold contradictions and oppositions, mentalities formed by tradition, and so forth. Marxism has not made nor can it make people immune to the influence of all these factors, nor has it endowed any of them with an "absolute" mentality independent of material processes. Like every ideology and all scientific knowledge, Marxism is a factor in social developments, but not their inner law. Therefore, Chinese policy is not what it is because it is based on Marxism, but because it is the reflection of a specific complex of objective and subjective factors in present-day Chinese society, as this has developed, or might have developed after the revolution. In that development the Marxist ideological orientation is only one of the major—and progressive—factors, but not the only one.

In other words, when, criticizing the foreign policies of other socialist countries from a "Marxist" standpoint, the Chinese theoreticians try to impose their conceptions of socialist international policy upon others, they do so by claiming to be the sole and exclusive interpreters of "true" Marxism. But in fact, all they do is force their policy upon others, a policy which is the result of specific Chinese social conditions and of the political trends arising from those conditions, which in this case are not in harmony with the ideological aims of socialism. For the very method by which this policy is being forced upon others—of which the Chinese anti-Yugoslav campaign is the most eloquent evidence—

points to the fact that the protagonists of this campaign are striving for a monopolistic leading role, ideological and political, in the socialist world, precisely in order to subordinate the interests of world socialism to their own political interests.

Let us first check the Chinese assertions by setting them against known arguments of classical Marxism and Leninism. Let me take the liberty of making more abundant use than might otherwise seem necessary of quotations from the works of Marx, Engels and Lenin, as well as some socialist spokesmen of our own day. This I do not do to prove that we and not the Chinese communists are the "only true Marxists", but to point to the fact that, from the point of view of Marxism, Chinese policy in certain of its specific aspects cannot be defended as a socialist policy, and particularly not as an efficacious or progressive socialist policy. However, although that policy cannot be defended as a "Marxist" policy, its causes and sources can be explained and its social-historical consequences seen precisely on the basis of Marxism.

CHAPTER 2

On Yugoslav "Opportunism" and Chinese "Radicalism"

The Chinese criticism of the communists of Yugoslavia begins with a criticism of their characteristics. The communists of Yugoslavia are afraid of war and imperialism, say these critics, and those of China are not afraid; *ergo,* since the former lack courage, they are for opportunism, and since the latter are brave, they are for a revolutionary radicalism. A classically "Marxist" interpretation of a policy, if ever there was one! And at the same time a very old and well-known method of concealing an extremely unrevolutionary trend by a pseudo-revolutionary phrase.

It looks as if the Chinese critics need to be reminded yet again of the fact—of which, for that matter they cannot possibly be ignorant—that the Yugoslav revolutionary workers' movement, headed by the Communist Party and Comrade Tito, was during the Second World War one of the very rare such movements which prepared, organized, and arms in hand with its own forces, that is, with the forces of its own people, carried a victorious socialist revolution through to the finish. This revolution the Communist Party of Yugoslavia carried through to the finish in the heart of Hitler's Europe, summoning the working masses not to peace but war, when the ruling bourgeoisie had already capitulated to the invader and proclaimed peace with him.

For victory under such circumstances not only were revolutionary ability and loyalty to the cause of socialism necessary, but also much heroism, and unshakable faith in the possibility of a revolutionary settlement of accounts with the fascist invader and the forces of reaction in Yugoslavia. For such a fight it was also necessary to have a profound internationalist faith in the indispensability of all-round support of the Soviet Union, as the main bastion of the revolution in its struggle against fascism. For this reason the Chinese critics can hardly hope to count on persuading the world that the cowardice and opportunism they allege are really characteristics of the communists of Yugoslavia.

Further, scarcely had the Yugoslav communists taken the first steps in the reconstruction of their war-devastated country—defending themselves simultaneously against the pressure of the reactionary forces abroad and at home, which wanted to crush the Yugoslav revolution by its own internal difficulties—when they found themselves faced with new difficulties caused and organized by Stalin's well-known pressure on Yugoslavia. Once again, for the Yugoslav communists not only to offer resistance to that pressure, but also to preserve the great achievements of the socialist revolution, to go on developing them and to consolidate their own compatriots' faith in the great future of socialist progress, it was necessary to possess not only much revolutionary ability and ideological firmness, but also courage too and a profound faith in the great internal strength of present-day socialism and its unquestionable ability to deal with all deformations in the development of the socialist countries and their policies. And this is precisely what the Yugoslav communists did succeed in achieving. For this reason the

Chinese critics will find it difficult to convince any fair-minded person that meek submission to alien pressure is a characteristic of the Yugoslav communists.

On the other hand, precisely this great and courageous revolutionary past of the Yugoslav communists and the experience they acquired in their own struggle, or observed in other people's struggles, has fitted them not to take any "infantile left-wing" complaint at its face value as proof of courage or the revolutionary spirit, or any empty radical phrase as a great revolutionary idea. Generally speaking any attempt at turning "radicalism" into a sort of absolute principle is in itself symptomatic of an unhealthy ideological condition. In practical politics such attempts are quite absurd, for they fail to take account of the actual conditions, and from the point of view of scientific socialism are senseless, not being based on an analysis of the actual relationships but on abstract ideological elaborations or even on mere wishes.

The mere fact of giving emphasis to such a principle amounts to a lapse into a static subjectivism. Of course, such a renunciation of dialectics subsequently acquires its own dialectical logic, for ultra-radicalism turns into pseudo-revolutionary phraseology coupled with impotence in practice, and pseudo-revolutionary phraseology is the mother of the most destructive sort of opportunism. Such phraseology serves to cover a sterile passivity and in practice a coming to terms with the unlimited power of the bourgeoisie, that is, with the elemental processes of development of the capitalist world. The communist parties which have suffered or today still suffer from this disease of radically-dyed opportunism, or sectarianism—which is the same thing—by reason of their "ultra-leftist" radicalism condemn themselves to isolation from reality and to impotence. This impotence and passivity in practice discredit them in the eyes of the working-class and of true revolutionaries. This is precisely why as a rule such parties abandon the political field and the working-class to the influence of other social and political forces and in this way in the ultimate effect of their policy completely identify themselves with opportunism.

In the history of the working-class movement pseudo-revolutionary radicalism in words has inflicted no little harm on the cause of the working-class and of socialism, probably not less than reformist opportunism. History—even the most recent—provides many examples of how parties and people guided by sterile radical phrases—under conditions not yet ripe for revolutionary action—become utterly incapable of any genuine revolutionary action when they really do find themselves in a situation which objectively calls for such action.

I could indeed cite more than one quite "fresh" example of the kind, but that would not serve any useful purpose. I would merely like to point to the fact that now the leaders of certain other communist parties are following the Chinese example and attacking us. Some of these leaderships have no achievements at all behind them which might give them the right to hand out to others lessons on the revolutionary spirit, and this for the simple reason that—in spite of their radicalism in words—having in practice failed to play a leading part, they have also shown themselves incapable of at least bringing their parties into the revolutionary and anti-imperialist actions begun without them. So now some of these dogmatic "radicals" in words—having found themselves outside the main current of revolution—have thought fit to give those who have already given proof of their revolutionary spirit in practice lessons about what is revolutionary and what is not. They obviously think that it will never "occur" to the working-class or the anti-imperialist forces that radicalism in words is no proof of a movement's being really revolutionary, let alone that such a movement is capable of leading the revolutionary process.

Only a policy which combines a clear revolutionary orientation with a realistic analysis of the objective conditions and of all the factors of social development is really revolutionary. This indeed is the real essence of scientific socialism. False "realism", of course, is often enough also an excuse for opportunism. But this in no way alters the fact that revolutions are born only under specific conditions and that the ability of communist parties consists not only in being able to make an objective evaluation of the conditions, but also to influence the creation of such conditions. They can do this only if they are able to link themselves with the broad body of the workers and influence the course of social development even when such revolutionary conditions do not yet exist. And for such an orientation the assumption is essential that when it is a question of processes within any individual country, the revolutionary transition from caditalism to socialism can in certain conditions be effected by means of armed revolution, but in other conditions also by a relatively peaceable political struggle.

As we know, it was precisely Lenin—ideologically responsible for the separation of the revolutionary workers' movement from the reformist wing of the Second International—who waged the most consistent and most uncompromising struggle against pseudo-revolutionary ultra-leftism. He constantly drew attention to the necessity of linking revolutionary enthusiasm with realism, to the need for concrete study of the facts, of the objective conditions of the situation, to the need for giving ear to the mood of the broad body of the people, to the indispensability of a revolutionary party's neither running ahead of, nor lagging behind that mood and so on, and it was precisely Lenin who in the sphere of socialist international policy offered the most resolute opposition to the ultra-leftist adventurism of Trotsky, who, under the slogan of world revolution was in fact prepared to plunge the Soviet Union into a war of adventure.

The true value and essence of the radicalism of the Chinese authors who attack Yugoslavia should be assessed not by their verbal radicalism but by the actual capability of their policy really to change conditions, that is, in the light of the results and final consequences of such a policy. Consequently, what we need first to clarify is the question whether this Chinese "ultra-radicalism" really is capable of strengthening the socialist and other progressive social forces and processes in the present-day world or not, that is, whether it does not even weaken these forces. Only the answer to this main question can give a final answer also to the question: whose policy is really revolutionary or, to put it more correctly, whose analyses of present-day realities and suitable aims for the forces of socialism are objective, the Chinese, or those other analyses which among others the Yugoslav communists make the starting-point of their policy.

However, let us first take a glance at whether the Chinese notions of a present-day foreign policy for socialism do necessarily derive from Marxism, in other words, whether it is the Yugoslav or the Chinese communists who in this field abandon certain fundamental socialist principles formulated by Marxism.

Of course, we are already used to being called revisionists and have long since stopped trying to prove to those who really have revised Marxism to the marrow that we are not revisionists. Comrade Tito once remarked that there are two revisionisms. This really is so. One revisionism revises the actual revolutionary and scientific bone-marrow of Marxism, forcing back the socialist forces either in the name of liberalism to bourgeois positions, or in the name of dogmatism to conservative bureaucratic *étatiste* positions. The other "revisionism" seeks the further development of the science of society in accordance with the conditions and needs of the present-day struggle to establish socialism, with precisely the revolutionary and scientific essence of Marxism and Leninism as starting point. Of this other "revisionism" we are not ashamed. On the contrary, we are proud if our revolution and our socialist development have in this respect made their modest contribution to the development of modern socialist scientific thought.

It is not my intention to defend the communists of Yugoslavia against the Chinese charges of revisionism. My aim is merely to point out the fact that Chinese "radicalism" can in no way be justified by Marxism.

CHAPTER 3

On the Inevitability of War

Only incurable petty-bourgeois pacifists could believe that war is not inevitable, say the Chinese critics of Yugoslavia. Only people whose heads are full of illusions or who deliberately aim at putting a good face on imperialism could assert that imperialism will renounce war, and, these same critics continue, only revisionists who have no faith in the vital strength and mind of man could assert that military technique can influence the course of social development. Of course all this is said to be handed down by the science of Marx, Engels and Lenin.

So first let us examine matters from that aspect.

Unfortunately for the Chinese theoreticians, in this respect the classics of Marxism have always been most clear. Even in their day, when it looked almost illusory to dream of a time when war would no longer be inevitable, Marx and Engels nevertheless did envisage such an age and possibility, though they did not tie them down to any dates in the historical process, but connected them with the maturing of a series of factors in the developments of society, both material and ideological-political, which would condition men's acts. In other words, on the one hand they did not envisage war's becoming impossible only when the last capitalist had vanished, nor on the other did they consider the victory of socialism in any country an absolute obstacle to war. As scientists and realists they knew that the victory of the revolution would not automatically make the socialist state faultless, so in the transitional period did not hold it to be impossible for even a socialist country to be responsible for a reactionary war.

It is utterly un-Marxist and unscientific when the Chinese theoreticians argue their thesis about the inevitability of war by the generalization—capitalism is inevitable war, socialism inevitable peace, therefore peace is feasible only if capitalism is completely eliminated. The problem can only be grasped completely if the concrete material and political factors and the quantitative relationships which at any given moment are decisive for war or peace are analysed as well as the prospects of their further development. Looked at in the abstract, the inevitability of war has never been absolute, fatal. It has always depended on the relationship of forces. And when Lenin pointed out that under the conditions of imperialism war was inevitable, because the imperialist factors inevitably "bred" war, what he was really thinking of was a relationship of forces in which the imperialist forces were superior, if not infinitely superior. Consequently it was really only a certain relationship of forces which made war inevitable in the circumstances of the absolute domination of imperialism. Whoever fails to grasp this will also be unable to see that the struggle for peace is in the circumstances of today precisely one of the means of struggle for *further change in the relationship of forces* in favour of peace and socialism, not for the petrification of the present relationship of forces. This, of course, supposing peace to be in the elementary interest of socialism, which the Chinese theoreticians also question.

Marx and Engels held wars to be an obstacle to the development of internal revolutionary movements and a brake on internal progressive social processes. Precisely for this reason they conceived the struggle against war and for disarmament to be an integral part of the struggle for democracy and socialism. Though without illusions about any "peaceableness" of capitalism or the bourgeoisie, they at the same time stood in opposition to those who considered war inevitable and demands for disarmament, illusions.

Here is what Engels wrote about the division of the Europe of his day into two large military camps (Russia and France on the one hand, Germany, Austria and Italy on the other), a passage which in fact was an envisagement of the coming world war:

"Both camps are getting ready for a decisive struggle —for a war such as the world has not yet seen, for a war in which from ten to fifteen million armed soldiers will face each other. Only two circumstances have so far prevented the explosion of that frightful war: first, the unprecedentedly rapid development of military technique, in which every newly invented form of weapon is superseded by new discoveries even before it can be introduced in a single army, and secondly, the absolute impossibility of calculating the odds, the complete uncertainty about who in the end would emerge the victor from that gigantic struggle.

All this danger of a world war would vanish the moment matters took such a turn in Russia that the Russian people could put an end to the traditional policy of conquest of their Tsars, and instead of dreaming of world domination, look after their own vital interests in their own country, interests threatened with extreme danger . . .

. . .Together with this any excuse for the mad armament which is turning all Europe into a military camp and forcing people to look upon war as a release, would vanish. Even the German Reichstag would then soon be compelled to put an end to its incessantly growing demands for money for war aims.

Thereby the West would attain the possibility, without any hindrances, of tackling the historical task which faces it in our time, that of resolving the conflict between the proletariat and the bourgeoisie and transforming capitalist society into socialist society."*[1]

And in another place Engels wrote:

"The system of standing armies has throughout Europe been brought to such a point that because of the burden of military expenditure it will either ruin the nations economically or take the monstrous form of a general war of destruction, unless the standing armies are transformed in time into a militia on the basis of a general arming of the whole nation.

I am trying to show that such a transformation is already possible now, even with the present-day governments and in the present-day political situation. Thus, starting from this situation, I propose only such measures that any government of today could adopt without harm to the defensive capabilities of its country. All I am trying to do is to establish that from a purely military standpoint there are absolutely no hindrances to the gradual curtailment of standing armies, or, in so far as these armies are nevertheless maintained, to

---

* Except where otherwise indicated, the passages quoted from other works in this book have been translated from the Serbo-Croat text used by the author.
[1] Marx-Engels: *Works*, Vol. XVI, Part 2, *Party Publishing House* of the Central Committee of the All-Union Communist Party (Bolsheviks), 1936, pp. 37-39.

doing this not for military but political reasons—in short, the purpose of the army being defence not so much against an external as an internal enemy."[1]

From all this the following conclusions are to be drawn:

1. Engels considered that wars and armament were a hindrance to the struggle for socialism.

2. Engels did not consider war to be fatally inevitable, but saw it as dependent on social changes in Russia, in other words, on a changed relationship of forces.

3. Noting this to be the position, Engels was not in favour of awaiting some sort of automatic change in the relationship of forces with folded arms, but of prompting that change by a struggle for a precise form of disarmament.

In other words, the theoreticians who proclaim the struggle for peace and disarmament to be an illusion and war advantageous to socialism, cannot find support in Marx or Engels.

Of course, dogmatically-minded critics will say that in his day Engels could not foresee the lines along which imperialism would develop, so was also unable properly to assess the role of war, standing armies or armaments. Of Lenin on the other hand they will say that he gave a complete analysis and evaluation of imperialism and by this was able to prove that in imperialism wars are inevitable.

More or less in the same sense Stalin in his time criticized Engels' article and held his analyses to be faulty. This of course was no accident, for, regarding the inevitability of war, Stalin too to a great extent fell into dogmatic ways of thinking. Nevertheless, there is a difference between present-

[1] Ibid., p. 337

34

day Chinese views and Stalin's. Although Stalin always emphasized that the inner contradictions of imperialism constituted factors favourable to the U.S.S.R., in practice he did underestimate the significance of those contradictions, and so in fact counted on the possibility of a united military action of the imperialist world against the U.S.S.R. Only that fact can explain the oscillation of Stalin's political orientation immediately before the Second World War. Stalin's orientation to the inevitability of war was in the first place the reflection of a defence policy which unquestionably had to be based on the fact that imperialism was still the ruling force in the world. Hence Stalin's critique of Engels' article, by which Stalin in fact wished to say that war was not dependent solely on changes in Russia, but also on changes in the West.

But independently of the question of whether or not Stalin's critique of Engels was justified, the fact that during and after the Second World War both circumstances and the relationship of forces were fundamentally changed, of itself means that the objective meaning of the dogma about the inevitability of war was also modified. In any case it ceases to be an argument for any defence policy, therefore can be distorted into a tendency towards the imposition of socialism from without by forcible means, thereby becoming a serious source of deformations of socialist international policy.

True, if viewed from the narrow angle of only a few decades, events have not borne Engels out. If however we see in them an adumbration of the direction that future movements will take, Engels' words ring differently today.

But even were we to consider that from a scientific standpoint Engels envisaged the future course of events wrongly—which, as I have said, would be unjustified, if we examine his assessments through the prism of a longer-term view—one should at the same time realize that Engels was a revolutionary, a political leader. He could not struggle against war while declaring it to be inevitable and could not fight against armaments while declaring them to be illusory. Only people unable to grasp the organic inner connection between opposites in movement could do that. War is inevitable if the forces of peace are too weak to prevent it. War can be prevented if the forces of peace overcome the forces of war. Consequently, *to speak of the inevitability of war—from the standpoint of Marxism—means one thing only: an objective appraisal that the relationship of forces between reaction and imperialism on the one hand and the working-class and the anti-imperialist forces on the other is such that this latter factor is unable to prevent war.* Whoever fails to make a factual analysis of this sort his starting-point, yet still talks about the inevitability of war, is indeed "afraid" of imperialism, that is to say, has no faith in his own forces or the forces of peace, that is to say, overestimates the forces of war and imperialism.

When they make their mechanical defence of the formula that "war is inevitable" do the Chinese critics make such a factual analysis of the relationship of forces their starting-point? No, they do not even mention it. In this regard they are satisfied with the propaganda phrase that imperialism is a "paper tiger". Consequently, their stubborn insistance that this "paper tiger" will nevertheless inevitably begin a war against the socialist camp simultaneously shows that they have not even got faith in their own propagandist phrase.

Instead of supporting their views by a factual Marxist analysis of the objective relationship of forces, they refer exclusively to quotations from Lenin, and this without any right at all, since it was precisely Lenin who most clearly formulated the attitude of socialism to war.

Lenin indubitably did say that imperialism inevitably breeds wars, but this thesis he also proved by a concrete analysis of internal social-economic movements in the epoch of imperialism. So doing he had in mind the following sorts of war: aggressive wars of conquest of other peoples, wars between powerful imperialist states waged over a redivision of the world, and wars against the socialist revolution, that is, against the first socialist country, the Soviet Union.

However, Lenin did not speak of the inevitability of those wars outside of space and time. It is one thing that imperialism as a system inevitably tends to war, that is, to trying by war to solve the contradictions which ravage it, but quite another whether it is able unhindered to realize those trends, or whether the relationship between the imperialist and the anti-imperialist forces is not such as to make imperialist wars more difficult or to prevent them altogether.

In Lenin's day—and particularly when Lenin was writing his well-known theoretical work on imperialism—the forces of imperialism exercised an unlimited sway over the world. Not only were the whole working-class and anti-imperialist movement incapable of preventing wars, it was not even theoretically possible to imagine that imperialism could overnight be prevented from acting according to its own objective inner laws.

The October Revolution was the first instance of a revolutionary working-class ending an imperialist war by a revolution, and thereby in practice proving that it was possible to struggle even against war. After this followed the second success: the working-class and people of the Soviet Union, with the support of the international working-class, its struggle and its revolutionary actions, succeeded in crushing the imperialist war of intervention in the Soviet Union, an achievement to which Lenin ascribed exceptional importance, precisely from the standpoint of appraisal of the new relationship of forces between imperialism and the anti-imperialistic forces, on the basis of which Lenin saw the feasibility of survival of the U.S.S.R. And finally, a third instance, Lenin spoke of the great historical significance of the agreement for peace concluded with bourgeois Esthonia, considering that this had definitely weakened the forces of imperialism and war.

Consequently, Lenin did not hold war to be a fatal inevitability so long as there was a vestige of imperialism in the world, but always viewed the matter on the basis of the relationship of forces. For this reason he did not see the struggle for peace—as the Chinese theoreticians do today—merely as a way of unmasking reactionaries and opportunists, but as a struggle for a concrete aim which corresponded to the expansion of socialism and hampered imperialism. Precisely for this reason he ascribed historical significance to the treaty of peace with Esthonia, just as he did to the contribution of the European proletariat in crushing intervention. For this reason the struggle for the further expansion of the socialist revolution and the struggle for the maintenance of the peaceable coexistence of the U.S.S.R. and the capitalist countries were to Lenin merely two facets of one and the same process.

Of course, Lenin knew that even when the civil war had ended the Soviet Union was relatively weak *vis-à-vis* the powerful imperialist states of the West. Nor did the process of a European revolution develop in the way that Lenin had previously hoped it would. Hence he was aware of the weakness of the anti-imperialist forces and of the danger of war, particularly against the U.S.S.R. But still he did not, like Trotsky, fatalistically fold his arms and regard war and world revolution as inevitable, but instead formulated a new Soviet foreign policy, based on long-lasting coexistence of the Soviet state and the capitalist states. His well-known thesis about the feasibility of building socialism in one state alone was the expression of this attitude of his. For what was this else but an expression of the conviction that it was possible to struggle against war, on the one hand by the consolidation of coexistence and on the other by the further development of the socialist revolution and anti-imperialist movements, by the further strengthening of the international working-class and its support of the Soviet Union and also by the further economic and political strengthening of the Soviet Union. In other words, although it was hard at that time to believe in the possibility of avoiding war between the Soviet Union and the capitalist world, Lenin did nevertheless admit the possibility of this. In the last resort history has confirmed Lenin's expectations. In the end the Second World War was after all not waged as a war of all the capitalist countries against the Soviet Union, but as the war of a coalition between that socialist country and a number of capitalist countries, against another coalition of capitalist countries. Thereby the thesis of coexistence passed an exceptionally difficult historical test. Why should something now suddenly become historically impossible which once before in history was possible?

What right, then, have the Chinese theoreticians to found their theories about the inevitability of war solely on those quotations from Lenin which are an expression of a concrete political situation, but not on Lenin's scientific views and principles concerning the connection between the question of war and the question of the quantitative relationship of social forces?

Consequently, the differences of opinion regarding the theory about the inevitability of war are not merely differences of opinion regarding the Marxist-Leninist interpretation of the problem of war and peace, but before all else have a deeper root in one or the other of the two following possibilities:

either the Chinese theoreticians believe that the relationship of forces in the world is such that the factors of imperialism not merely wish to impose war on the world, with prospects of winning, but are also capable of doing so;

or the Chinese theoreticians consider that war is in the interests of socialism, that is to say, that it is the "revolutionary weapon" of socialism, and consequently the growth of the forces of socialism of itself makes war inevitable.

In the first instance, overestimating the forces of imperialism, they deny their own theory about the "paper tiger". In the second case they are venturing on to a very dangerous and very slippery road, which leads to the complete deformation of socialist international policy and of the relationship between the nations on the socialist road.

For this reason we need to examine both these possibilities.

CHAPTER 4

The Present-Day Quantitative Relationship of the Social Forces and War

If the Chinese theoreticians cannot find any support in Lenin for their way of understanding the theory of the inevitability of war, still less can they find any in the actual facts of the realities of today. Since Lenin's time the quantitative relationship of the social forces in the world has changed so profoundly that we can without any exaggeration say that the problem of war and coexistence is now quite different from what was in Lenin's day.

The world of today is not that of yesterday. A great number of anti-imperialist factors which in Lenin's time were still extremely undeveloped now constitute a tremendous force, both material and political.

First, the forces of socialism have grown greatly. There are a number of socialist states. These are not merely a significant political factor, but are becoming an ever more influential economic fact in the world of today. Not only do they influence the development of political relations between peoples, but also the development of economic relations, in the sense of introducing new elements and forms into those relations, a process still only at its beginning, but which in course of time will steadily become an ever more important factor in international economic cooperation.

41

At the same time the social role and the influence of the working-class are steadily strengthening. The working-class is linking to itself ever wider circles of progressively and democratically disposed people. In no case is it interested in the maintenance of a policy of aggressive war, and—however split up it may be ideologically—this it will not support except if the socialist countries themselves, through their own errors, help reactionary and aggressive circles to make out war to be the unavoidable defence of national independence. In addition, waging war against the will of the working-class is in the conditions of today becoming increasingly difficult.

Further, the last remains of colonial empires and classical colonialism are crumbling before our eyes. True, imperialist tendencies are making every effort to find an outlet in some other way, that is, by the imposition of varied forms of economic and political "influence", but none the less it remains a fact that the economic basis of imperialism has now been so reduced that the struggle for the political and economic division of the world is coming up against limits which are narrower and narrower and ever more resistant. On the one hand those limits are formed by the forces of socialism, and on the other by peoples who have liberated themselves or are still liberating themselves from imperialist dependence and are striving towards their economic independence. Not only does this process hamper the forces of imperialism and war in their foreign expansion, but it also has an increasingly powerful influence on the internal social development of the capitalist countries.

Further, the role of imperialist contradictions between the large capitalist states has been quantitatively changed.

In Lenin's day those contradictions reigned supreme and in practice made the contradictions *vis-à-vis* the first socialist country secondary, as was seen in the course of the Second World War. Now the situation has changed. The imperialist contradictions between the large capitalist states are narrowed down and reduced to a secondary role, that is, are dependent on the development and method of resolution of what are now the basic contradictions, that is, of the contradictions between the world of socialism and the world of capitalism. And this means that war is not dependent merely on the internal laws of the development of capitalism but also on the internal laws of the development of socialism.

Parallel with all these changes, which have established new quantitative relations between the social forces in the world, yet another factor has appeared which acts in the same sense, and this is the revolutionary advance in science and technology which has fundamentally changed the whole strategy and tactics of any possible world war. New military equipment which is terrifyingly destructive and is now concentrated and shared between the two poles of the dominant world contradiction, has brought about a specific balance between the material forces of these two poles. This balance resides in the fact that the destructive force of any possible future world war is such that both victory and defeat would produce practically equal material and social-political consequences. Thereby in a certain sense military equipment itself becomes an obstacle to war. It constitutes such a danger of world destruction that nobody, even if equipped with great power, would easily find a new world war profitable. It looks as if history has in this field been at pains to strike a balance between people's subjective aspirations and the degree of social consciousness and the material conditions, leaving less and less room for personal decisions in this field.

And finally, the feeling that things cannot go on any longer in the old way has a great influence also on the inner political differentiation of bourgeois society. If the policy of the socialist countries were unambiguously set on a course for peace and coexistence, not only would the socialist forces in those countries inevitably be strengthened, but also the aspirations for a peaceable understanding and agreement with the countries of socialism, and this not only in the working-class, but also in the broadest ranks of the nation, including here considerable portions of the bourgeoisie. In other words, under such conditions it will be precisely the inner social and political process that will be the most powerful defence against the triumph of aggressive tendencies.

The fact is, the whole imperialist system, as a system, is breaking up. By this I do not mean to say that imperialism is no longer a powerful factor, or rather, that it no longer constitutes a danger as the instigator of a new world war, but that it is quite certain that those possibilities are being increasingly reduced, and—for a certain time—can be reduced to a minimum, providing the socialist forces have an appropriate policy.

It goes without saying that only the policy of coexistence can be the appropriate policy here, the policy, that is to say, which should ensure all nations a right to independent development and free them to the maximum from any fear of anybody's interference from outside. Today it is feasible to rally the vast majority of mankind on such a platform,

44

for the determined defence of peace in the world. If the socialist forces pursue such a policy, war is not inevitable. But were they to pursue a policy which lumped all that was non-communist into a single camp opposed to socialism, that is to say, prompted the grouping of the world into fronts set for a "definitive" decision, war could become inevitable. Herein lies the greatest danger of the Chinese theory about the inevitability of war. In other words, *the fate of the world does not depend only on the strength or will of imperialism but also on the policy and subjective views of the decisive socialist factors.*

However, from the theses of the Chinese authors it would seem that nothing has changed in the world since Marx or Lenin's day.

"Wherever we look"—say the Chinese theoreticians —"not one new branch of technology, such as atomic energy, rockets, etc., has, as the modern revisionists assert, changed the basic features of the epoch of imperialism and the proletarian revolution to which Lenin drew attention."[1]

These words are a typical example of how incapable certain Chinese authors of such theories are of grasping the dialectics of movement, or the organic inner connection between evolution and revolution. Since they look at things statically, they fail to see that the process of change of the qualitative relationships runs precisely along the course of change of the quantitative relationships. Of course, modern technology has not changed the essence of imperialism, but by making it more difficult for war to break out it has diminished the force of imperialism, speeded up the process

[1] *The Red Flag*, according to the *Hsinhua Agency* bulletin of April 9, 1960.

of its internal disintegration and created more favourable objective conditions for the struggle for socialism and the further consolidation of peace. And these quantitative changes unquestionably are of significance; if nothing else, at least they go to show that there are new circumstances in the struggle for socialism and social progress as a whole in the world.

However, the Chinese theoreticians have subordinated dialectics too, the objective laws of movement of society, to themselves, or rather, to their present policy. So they have harnessed the philosophy of Marxism too to the cart of their anti-Yugoslav campaign. Here is what they say:

"The materialist dialectic considers that the struggle between opposites is absolute, while the unity is relative. If we speak of their essential differences, these opposites determine the definite line of demarcation which cannot be ignored solely because of their unity and mutual transformation. This is one of the main themes of the Marxist science. The Marxist-Leninist teaching about the class struggle is precisely the practical application of this theoretical principle.

But present-day revisionism does not admit this revolutionary theoretical principle. It destroys the essential distinction between the two opposites, as if the struggle between them were not absolute and as if the unity of contradictions were absolute. This sophistic attitude is exactly reflected in a revisionist attitude towards the class struggle, particularly the international class struggle."[1]

1 From an article by Chang Pei: *A Criticism of the Sophism of Present-Day Revisionism*, published in the monthly magazine *Theory and Practice*, No. 9, of September 15, 1958.

The first sentence here is Lenin's, but as it has been plucked out of its context, it does not express Lenin's full thought. All the following sentences, further, are really a distortion of the sense of the first sentence. First, we must point out that Lenin's reflections have been directly distorted, for, quoting Lenin's thesis from the *Philosophical Notebooks*, the author simply ignores an "N.B." which Lenin added, which runs:

"The unity (coincidence, identity, resultant) of opposites is conditional, temporary, transitory, relative. The struggle of mutually exclusive opposites is absolute, just as development and motion are absolute.

N. B. The distinction between subjectivism (scepticism, sophistry, etc.) and dialectics, incidentally, is that in (objective) dialectics the difference between the relative and absolute is itself relative. For objective dialectics there is an absolute even *within* the relative. For subjectivism and sophistry the relative is only relative and excludes the absolute."[1]

Explanation is unnecessary. What Lenin wrote here could serve as an accurate appraisal of the philosophy of Chang Pei, and Chang Pei certainly had his reasons for quoting only the first part of Lenin's thesis, not the second.

However, it is not a matter of the philosophy, but of its practical sense. In fact, twisting the sense of Lenin's thesis that the unity of opposites is relative, while the conflict of opposites is absolute, the Chinese author—deliberately or unwittingly—draws the practical conclusion that *the poles* opposed to each other and *the forms* of struggle between them are absolute and unchangeable. By this he

Lenin: *Selected Works*, International Publishers, New York, Vol. XI, p. 82.

desires to show that nothing in the world has changed, and that if nothing has changed, the relative character of the unity of contradictions conditions ever sharper forms of conflict between the two opposites. Were things like this, the policy of coexistence and any policy of peace would directly aid the maintenance of the existing state of things in the capitalist countries.

However, the sense of Lenin's theses is quite different from this. To Lenin what is absolute is—the movement of things. What the Chinese theoreticians on the other hand understand as absolute is an immutability of the factors and forms of contradiction, whatever the quantitative changes that may arise in the inner relationship of forces. Here in fact all movement ceases, and with it dialectics, and subjectivism and statical dogmatism begin.

Perhaps it is rather pointless to enter into polemics about Marxist dialectics with these Chinese theoreticians, for they need the passages from philosophical theses which they cite solely as one supporting argument more for their particular political schemes, for their practical line of action. Yet when it comes to dragging Marxist philosophy into a most shabby hostile political campaign, perhaps one should after all say a word more about this Chinese philosophy.

The fact is, as the Chinese theoreticians who criticize Yugoslav "revisionism" see things, everything is static, forms and poles of contradiction do not change at all, nor do the weapons of the struggle change. According to such a conception of dialectics, all that changes is the sharpness of the contradictions, and it is in this way that at a given stage things come to a revolutionary transformation. And this process, through all time, so long as socialism and capitalism last, and in all countries, is—according to these views—bound to be repeated in the same way.

However, the dialectical process of movement is much more complex. Quantitative changes in regard to contradictions are inevitably reflected in qualitative changes within the poles of those contradictions. And those qualitative changes at the same time produce new quantitative relationships. In this indeed lies the very process of constant change, both of the very nature of the unity of contradictions and of the means and forms of struggle within the opposites. All that is constant is the struggle itself, until at last a new qualitative condition arises, while everything else constantly develops and changes, which is precisely what constitutes the movement of things. Losing sight of all this, the Chinese authors are in fact in the same anti-dialectic position of static, subjectivistic viewing of the development of social movements in which Stalin was when he postulated the theory that as the class enemy weakened, class contradictions grew sharper and sharper.

When one contemplates philosophy of that sort, inevitably one recalls Engels' words :

"To the metaphysician, things and their mental images, ideas, are isolated, to be considered one after the other apart from each other, rigid, fixed objects of investigation given once for all. He thinks in absolute irreconcilable antithesis. His communication is, 'Yea, yea. Nay, nay, for whatsoever is more than these cometh of evil.' For him a thing either exists or it does not exist; it is equally impossible for a thing to be itself and at the same time something else. Positive and negative absolutely exclude one another; cause and effect stand in equally rigid antithesis one to the other.

At first sight this mode of thought seems to us extremely plausible, because it is the mode of thought of so-called sound common sense. But sound common sense, respectable fellow as he is within the homely precincts of his own four walls, has most wonderful adventures as soon as he ventures out into the wide world of scientific research. Here the metaphysical mode of outlook, justifiable and even necessary as it is in the domains whose extent varies according to the nature of the object under investigation, nevertheless sooner or later always reaches a limit beyond which it becomes one-sided, limited, abstract, and loses its way in insoluble contradictions. And this is so because in considering individual things it loses sight of their connections; in contemplating their existence it forgets their coming into being and passing away; in looking at them at rest it leaves their motion out of account; because it cannot see the wood for the trees."[1]

This is an accurate picture of the methods of the Chinese critics of the Yugoslav concepts of the struggle for socialism. Precisely for this reason, the greatest sin of the Yugoslav "revisionists", according to Chinese ideas, is in their assertion that since the times of Marx and Lenin the world has continued to change, that capitalism has changed in many features, and that socialism too has changed in many features—these changes, of course, taking place in two different directions.

Even while I write these words I can hear the chorus of dogmatic article-writers replying in unison that here I am again putting a pretty face on capitalism and imperialism.

---

[1] F. Engels: *Anti-Dühring*, Cooperative Publishers, Moscow, 1934, p. 28.

50

But here I am not discussing the ethical behaviour of imperialism or capitalism or their aesthetic appearance, for this
has not essentially changed at all. If it has changed in some
respects, it was indeed—as the Chinese theoreticians always
insist—obliged to change, under the pressure both of economic development and the strengthening of the socialist
and other progressive forces. But whether "compelled" or
"not compelled", the historical result is the same. "Com-
pulsion" of that sort is indeed one of the laws of history.
But in no sense is this the main question. What I am suggesting here is something different, namely, that the strength
of capitalism and imperialism is today relatively incompa-
rably less in ratio to the forces of socialism than in the days
when Lenin wrote about the inevitability of imperialist
wars, and further, that this capitalist, imperialist system is
now subject to rapid internal decay, so that whether that
process will be speeded up or braked depends to a great
extent on the policy of the socialist forces being an appropriate one. And the process can be braked not only by reformist opportunism but also by pseudo-revolutionary radicalism, particularly by anything that looks at all like a sort
of "socialist Bonapartist adventurism".

A typical example of a subjectivist and un-Marxist
approach to the problems of the world of today is the way
in which certain Chinese authors attacked Comrade Tito
when on a certain occasion he spoke of the influence of
modern war technology on the development of international
relations, in the sense quoted above.

Tito drew the conclusion that modern war technology
makes it more difficult for war-mongers to provoke a war,
that is, makes the struggle for peace a more feasible one.

But to Tito's thesis the Chinese critics replied that Tito was trying to frighten them with imperialist war technology, but forgot that it is man that is everything, that is, that the mind of man can overcome any technology.

Here we need to point to two aspects of such Chinese criticisms.

First of all, every man knows—and certainly we Yugoslav communists do, having had rich experience in that respect—that the man who fights for his ideal with full consciousness can overcome even a more powerful enemy and more powerful equipment. But it is not whether or not the socialist nations would be able to win with poorer armament that is at stake here—in itself anyway a completely unreal supposition—but whether, in a situation in which both sides dispose of such tremendous war techniques, the capitalist countries could find it worth while to engage in a war of aggression.

Of course, the matter stands differently if we are to take these Chinese propaganda arguments against Tito's objective analyses as meaning that the Chinese authors think that precisely the socialist countries should engage in a war of conquest against the non-socialist countries. This would mean that the stronger the socialist world, the more war would be inevitable. But in that case the Chinese theoreticians should not deceive themselves: they would not have those ideological advantages which make any form of armament victorious, it would be the others who possessed them. This is convincingly shown by the case of Napoleon.

The other aspect of these Chinese criticisms is that they altogether deny the influence of war techniques as of any other technique on the course of social development.

Precisely for this reason the Chinese article-writers reply to Tito's objective observation by shallow political propagandist catch-phrases. And while they thus deny the influence of the development of war techniques on the treatment of the question of the inevitability of war, the Chinese theoreticians refer back to Marxism and Leninism. Let us set their assertion against passages from Marx, Engels and Lenin.

Here is one of Marx's pronouncements:

"The recruitment of the whole population able to bear arms into armies that could be counted in millions, and the introduction of firearms, projectiles and explosives of hitherto undreamt-of efficacy created a complete revolution in warfare. This, on the one hand, put a sudden end to the Bonapartist war period and insured peaceful industrial development, since any war other than a world war of unheard-of cruelty and absolutely incalculable outcome had become an impossibility."[1]

Consequently, while the Chinese theoreticians deny the influence of the development of war technology on the course of social development, Marx ascribed to it nothing short of an epoch-making significance.

Discussing the development of war technology and the influence of that development on social developments and the future of war as a means of resolving contradictions, Engels wrote the following:

"We, on the contrary, have absolutely no cause for annoyance when we see that, in this competition between armour-plating and guns, the warship is being developed

[1] Marx-Engels: *Selected Works*, International Publishers, New York, Vol. II p. 180.

to a pitch of perfection which is making it both outrageously costly and unusable in war,[1] and that this struggle makes manifest also in the sphere of naval warfare those immanent dialectical laws of motion on the basis of which militarism, like all other historical phenomena, is being brought to destruction as a result of its own development".[2]

Thus Engels too ascribed great significance to the influence of war techniques on social development, so great a significance that in his opinion that development by its own dialectics of development constituted one of the decisive factors leading to the elimination of war as an instrument in the relations between the nations. What is more, he held that the development of war techniques also influenced other forms of the class struggle. Here is what he said about this:

"If the conditions have changed in the case of war between nations, this is no less true in the case of the class struggle. The time of surprise attacks, of revolutions carried through by small politically conscious minorities at the head of the politically unconscious masses, is past. Where it is a question of a complete transformation of the social organizations, the masses themselves must also be in it, must themselves already have grasped what is at stake, what they are going in for."[3]

Possibly the Chinese authors consider that in this respect Engels was wrong. But even if he was wrong, in any case

---

[1] It looks as if this will be realized by the perfection of the latest product of heavy industry for naval warfare—the automatic torpedo, for with this the smallest torpedo-boat would be more powerful than the largest dreadnought.
[2] F. Engels: *Anti-Dühring*, Cooperative Publishers, Moscow, 1934, English edition, p. 197.
[3] Marx-Engels: *Selected Works*, International Publishers, New York, Vol. II p. 187.

it is plain that the Chinese authors have not got any right to refer back to Marxism for support of their denial of the role of war technology on social developments.

We however consider that in principle Engels was right. Of course, processes of that sort do not unfold independently of the results of the political struggle for socialism or of the actual development of socialism. But the same factors prompt development in both one and the other direction, transforming all those movements into a single integrated process of development.

Developed socialist relationships are possible solely on the basis of highly developed technology, which of itself makes wars more difficult to engage in, since it makes them more destructive. The victor has no material advantage to expect from so destructive a war. Apart from this, the development of socialism—precisely because of highly developed technology, which calls for an all-embracing international division of labour and thereby creates a sense of the common interests of all mankind—means a constant growth of a sense of the equality of all men independently of language or race. Thereby war becomes ever less acceptable from the standpoint both of the political and the ethical views of all men and all nations.

The maturing of both these factors—that is, the maturing of technology and the development of socialism—thus results in wars ceasing to be, not only inevitable, but also—at a certain stage of development—becoming impossible.

It was clearly precisely of these facts that Lenin was thinking in reflections such as the following, which N. K. Krupskaia describes :

"It should be said that Vladimir Ilich was fond on occasion of peering into the distance and dreaming about the future. I recall a conversation we had about war. This was in Leningrad, early in 1918. Vladimir Ilich remarked that modern technology in our day was increasingly furthering the destructive character of war. But the time would come when war would be so destructive that it would become quite impossible. Later, in 1920 and 1921 Vladimir Ilich returned again to this question. He told me about a talk he had had with an engineer who had said that there already existed an invention such that it would be feasible to destroy a whole army at a distance. This would make any war impossible. Of this Ilich spoke with great enthusiasm. It was clear that he passionately desired war to become impossible. Ilich took the question of war in process of change. Whatever question he touched upon, he never considered any phenomenon in a petrified aspect."[1]

One merely needs to compare these prophetic words with the conservatism of thought of the Chinese authors who, repeating phrases of Lenin torn from speeches and articles written regarding concrete political set-ups, draw conclusions about the inevitability of wars. for it to be clear how little and how indifferently these Chinese make use of Marxism and Leninism. This of course is no accidental phenomenon. However much they may be garbed in Marxist phraseology, their theories serve quite clearly-defined social-political purposes. This is why in Chinese conditions Marxism is "modified" in a specific manner.

But let us return to the analysis of the quantitative relationship of the social forces and the influence of this

---

[1] N. K. Krupskaia: *About Lenin*, Moscow, 1960, pp. 40—41.

on the problem of the inevitability of war. Through the prism of those relationships let us examine all three possible forms of imperialist war.

From the standpoint of military techniques and all other conditions, war for the conquest of other peoples is still not only possible but, in certain conditions, relatively the least risky for the aggressor. Nevertheless, practical examples of the collapse of colonial empires and like phenomena indicate that the possibilities of such wars and the chances of success in them are becoming increasingly less. This is unquestionably the consequence of the growth of anti-imperialist resistance among the oppressed peoples, of a strengthening of the feeling of national independence and of equality, and a strengthening of the socialist forces and their support and of democratic resistance within the capitalist countries. We can with justice assume that all these anti-imperialist factors will grow stronger, and this means that in the future it will be increasingly more difficult to start even local wars for the enslavement of other peoples.

The second kind of imperialist war, that is, war between the large imperialist states themselves, waged for a new division of the world, to all intents became obsolete during the Second World War. However the imperialist contradictions inside the capitalist world develop in the future, the basic contradiction of the world of today—the contradiction between the world of socialism and the world of capitalism—has to such an extent reduced them to the state of being a secondary factor that the possibility of wars breaking out between the large capitalist countries for a new division of the world has been reduced to a theoretical minimum such that in political practice it scarcely needs considering.

By this, it goes without saying, I do not mean to assert that capitalist contradictions no longer exist. They do exist, but they are so weakened, and the forms through which they manifest themselves are so changed that they are no longer capable alone, independently, of being resolved by war—except in various forms of local wars on other people's backs—but are instead connected up with the basic contradiction of the world of today, the contradiction between socialism and capitalism.

After all this can the Chinese theoreticians still assert that nothing has changed in the question of the inevitability of war? If they have any trace of respect for objective fact, they could not do so. If nevertheless they do, they certainly have other reasons for it.

And finally, the third kind of imperialist war—an aggressive war against the socialist states. Such a war is not only possible, but even has its protagonists in the most reactionary and war-mongering circles of the capitalist world. Admittedly, among them there are not very many who would be openly for war under present-day conditions, for the majority of them are aware that today aggressive war has no prospects of achieving victory. But there are many more who, like the Chinese communists, consider war inevitable, so continue to keep the iron hot in the fire, in the hope that time will change things to their advantage.

However, counter to those tendencies and circles there also exists all that tremendous material and political strength of the factors of peace, of progress, of socialism in the world and inside those countries of which we spoke above. There is no reason whatsoever to suppose that these factors will become weaker in the future. On the contrary, they will grow stronger and develop an increasingly powerful influence on the course of world events. To believe that in such circumstances war is inevitable is either seriously to overestimate the force of the factor of imperialism or seriously to underestimate the strength of socialism and of the other anti-imperialist factors.

We do neither. We are not inclined to underestimate the strength of the imperialist factors. For this reason we consider it the indispensable duty of all nations and all peace-loving forces to struggle actively for peace and for the suppression of all aggressive tendencies. But we are also not inclined to underestimate the strength of the progressive and peace-loving factors, which are becoming ever more capable of eliminating any chance of the aggressor's succeeding in a war.

In other words, for war to cease to be inevitable it is not necessary for the last corner of the world to be socialist, *but for the material and ethical-political forces of socialism and peace to be so strong that they are able to prevent any attempt to resolve the imperialist and other international contradictions by a world war, which will at the same time speed up the attempt to resolve those contradictions by internal means and internal forms of political and economic struggle within every country.*

What support then remains for the Chinese theory of the inevitability of war at the present time? There remains only one more theoretical possibility, the supposition that the socialist countries might adopt the line of finding in war a solution to the contradiction between the world of socialism and the world of capitalism. This would mean the deliberate adoption by the socialist countries of a policy of a war of conquest. However, such trends would both ideologically and in practice be in complete opposition to the aims of socialism and its elementary interests both today and tomorrow. For this reason there is little likelihood of their finding support in the socialist world, which we can best see from the fortune of the theories of the Chinese authors which we are discussing here.

However, the very fact that such trends could appear and—deliberately or unconsciously—be expressed by precisely the same Chinese writers who attack the policy of coexistence is eloquent proof that it is not only the capitalist countries that bear responsibility for the maintenance of peace. In circumstances when the socialist system has become a world force, but still possessing vestiges of the old views and egoistic and other such tendencies, the phenomenon is not excluded of some country on the socialist road— because of certain specific inner conditions—yielding to the temptation to make use of the strength of socialism, not only for its defence but also for an attempt to achieve certain aims which have no connection whatsoever with socialism. Consequently, proportionately to the growth of the power of the socialist countries also grows their responsibility for peace, a responsibility of all socialist forces.

At the present time material and social-political conditions are increasingly maturing which prevent war. If such possibilities exist, the socialist forces have only one choice— to struggle to see that feasibility, that is, the feasibility of the preservation of peace, is exploited to the utmost. For this reason they must oppose those trends within the socialist world which act in the opposite direction, and among these is not only the anti-communist campaign of certain social-democratic circles, but also this campaign against the very policy of coexistence, and against Yugoslavia in particular which—together with a line asserting the inevitability of war— is pursued by leading circles of the Communist Party of China.

There is no doubt but that socialism will master ultra-radical trends of this sort, which whether those who put them forward wish this or not in fact lead to a war of conquest. That those trends cannot find a fertile soil today, the development and role of the Soviet Union, as the greatest socialist force, is prime evidence. Here it is not merely the concrete foreign policy acts of the Soviet Union that are decisive, but above all the significant material and social-political results of present-day Soviet internal development, which have come to expression so markedly during the past few years. These results today are such that by themselves, that is, to a great extent independently of personal factors, they prompt the further advance of socialist social relationships, and thereby also make the implementation of the adventurist trend of which I have spoken impossible.

It goes without saying that it is not only the Soviet Union that is responsible for peace, but also every other socialist country and all the socialist forces in the world together with them. Those socialist and progressive movements—outside the communist—which are frequently led astray by various anti-communist slogans, by which they not only play into the hands of the forces of bourgeois reaction, but also the forces of war, also bear responsibility. The international policy of socialism is the result of the action of all the factors of the working-class and anti-imperialist forces. This is precisely what should never be forgotten, and certainly not in any serious Marxist analysis.

CHAPTER 5

The Policy of Coexistence and Marxism

In the circumstances of today the struggle for peace is above all simultaneously part of the struggle for socialism. This means that we have still more reason to make a completely realistic assessment of all the horrors of destruction that a new world war would bring mankind, so as to do still more to rally all peoples to the struggle for peace.

But no, the Chinese theoreticians are annoyed by such declarations. They do not like a future war to be spoken of in terms that are too black, for, they say, this merely frightens people, whereas it is only imperialists whom we should frighten. In their view to be against war and talk about its consequences is to be afraid of war. Whereas—in the same view—one should not be afraid of war, because its "sacrifices will be soon redeemed", since after the war at least half mankind will survive, and survive in a state of well-being never seen before. Here is what they say about this:

"We are consistently opposed to the provoking of criminal wars by imperialism, for an imperialist war would cause the peoples of the various countries (including the peoples of the U.S.A. and of other imperialist countries) great sacrifices. Nevertheless, were the imperialists to insist on imposing such sacrifices on the nations, we are convinced that those sacrifices would soon be redeemed, as the experience of the Russian and the Chinese revolutions has shown. On the ruins of dead imperialism the victorious peoples will soon build up a civilization at a level a thousand times higher than the capitalist system, and a future for themselves which would be really glorious."[1]

"The revolutionary peoples constitute more than nine-tenths of the population of the world. It is open to anybody to see into whose hands the fruits of the struggle will fall—those of the revolutionary peoples, who constitute more than nine-tenths of the world population, or those of the imperialists and reactionaries of various countries, who constitute less than ten percent. Anybody can see for himself who in the end will be the master of the world."[2]

Anybody who counts on the normal reasoning of men and the elementary aspirations of the people must find this cold-blooded calculating logic with which the Chinese politicians discuss war completely alien and unacceptable. In his time Lenin wrote:

"We know, and know very well, too, what unheard-of misfortunes war brings the workers and peasants. For this reason it is our duty to approach this question cautiously and attentively. We are making the maximum of concessions and sacrifices, our only aim is to preserve the peace which we have bought at such great cost."[3]

What a tremendous difference between these statements! And when it comes to the consequences of present-day war, what should one not say? Clearly it is not a question of whether anybody is or is not afraid of war, but whether

---

[1] *Red Flag*, according to the *Hsinhua Agency*, Peking, April 19, 1960.
[2] Leading article in *Jen min ji bao* of June 29, 1960.
[3] Lenin: *Works*, 4th Russian edition, Vol. XXX, p. 122.

he is against war or for war, that is, whether he is doing all he can to see that war is prevented, or is not doing this, but would even rather like a war to take place. And the key to the determination of any person's attitude to war is precisely his attitude towards the problem of the coexistence of states with different social systems.

Of course, if a man's attitude is that war is fatefully inevitable, the policy of coexistence is in his way. For this reason it is precisely this principle of Yugoslav foreign policy that has been submitted to the fiercest Chinese critics' attacks.

The problem of the feasibility or non-feasibility of the policy of coexistence is closely connected in the first place with the question of how far the proposition that today wars are no longer inevitable is realistic. If war is inevitable, coexistence is an unfeasible fiction, an illusion. In other words, proving that war is inevitable is simultaneously to prove that the policy of coexistence is unfeasible, consequently is mistaken and harmful to the cause of socialism. And indeed, in the work of Chinese theoreticians today we do find, appropriately enough, this very argument further buttressed by appeals to "true" Marxism. And the target of attack in this question is Yugoslavia, so that Yugoslavia should be used for a political battle waged generally against the policy of peaceable coexistence and peace.

Of course, since the policy of coexistence is the policy of the socialist camp, the Chinese writers insist that our coexistence is different from that of the socialist camp. At times the Chinese authors, in words, are in favour of peaceable coexistence, but not in favour of the same sort of coexistence as the Yugoslav communists'. Since of course the difference between one sort of coexistence and the other—that is, the coexistence which the Chinese are in favour of and that which the Yugoslavs want—cannot be defined by any sort of scholastic argument—for coexistence either is or is not—the "arguments" about the differences boil down to common insinuations.

Real differences of opinion of course do exist. But they do not reside in any conception of the "quality" of coexistence, but in the fact that the Yugoslav communists stand for a policy of coexistence, while the arguments of the Chinese theoreticians show that in reality they are against it. According to the Chinese theoreticians the sin of the Yugoslavs is in the fact that they assert that the policy of coexistence is a lasting one, a fundamental element of socialist international policy, while in the Chinese view coexistence can be no more than a transitory state, which sooner or later will be terminated either by imperialism or by the socialist forces, which have no reason fundamentally to renounce war for the destruction of imperialism. In addition to this, of course, these critics add that the Yugoslav policy of coexistence amounts to propaganda for the *status quo* between the enslavers and the enslaved, the exploiters and the exploited and so forth, while of their own "policy of coexistence" they assert that it is based on the future revolutionary collapse of imperialism, for which reason it is equally inevitably a transitory policy, a temporary one, seeing that a war against imperialism is inevitable.

There is no need for any special underlining that such a view of the policy of coexistence in fact means the negation of that policy. For there is no need to fight for temporary coexistence. We have it. The real question is whether the conditions for lasting peaceable coexistence exist, either while there are states with varying social systems in the world or when there are not. The Chinese theories deny such a possibility, consequently they deny the very policy of coexistence, proclaiming it to be unfeasible, an illusion.

As everybody knows, for Yugoslav communists the justification of the policy of coexistence is based on the following:

1) on the conviction that in the circumstances of today it will be ever more difficult for the forces of imperialism and war to break the existing coexistence, which will bring the internal contradictions and oppositions of the capitalist world to a new stage of development, that is, it will speed up the processes of disintegration of imperialism and capitalism as a system and increasingly strengthen the part played by socialist factors, material and political;

2) on the conviction that the imposing of socialism on other nations from outside by war is a harmful and profoundly anti-socialist conception, behind which can be—and inevitably will be—hidden all manner of hegemonistic and reactionary trends, apart from which the socialist countries' assumption of responsibility for a frightfully destructive world war, in order to "make others happy" by force, would profoundly compromise the very concept of socialism and lend imperialism and all the vestiges of the old world new strength.

In other words, *the policy of coexistence is the expression of our conviction that in the circumstances of today warmongering circles in the capitalist world are going to find it increasingly more difficult to force a new world war on mankind, while the socialist world in principle and in practice rejects, or should reject, the very notion of a war of conquest as the*

66

instrument for forcing socialism on others. Since we conceive of the policy of coexistence in this way, it of course must necessarily either be a permanent principle of socialist international policy or not be at all.

This of course does not mean that we see the policy of coexistence as a rigid dogma. Nobody can foresee with precision what actual groupings in the relationship of world social forces will appear in the course of further developments. Nor can anybody foresee all the numerous instruments or all the multifarious forms in which and through which the future struggle for the final establishment of socialist relationships will unfold, any more than one can foresee the future forms of mutual aid of the socialist forces. But one thing remains, as a sacred principle: the imposition of socialism or of any of its forms by aggression from without will always be alien to socialism, an unacceptable and reactionary instrument. The elimination of that instrument is indeed the long-term purpose of the policy of coexistence.

That the Chinese conceptions of coexistence cannot be defended by Marxism is not difficult to prove. True, Marx and Engels did not specially deal with the matter, or at any great length, for in their time this problem did not look either acute or important. Nevertheless, from all that they wrote it is easy to grasp that it never even entered their heads that the expansion of socialism could go by any other path than that of the internal social processes of each country. There is no evidence that Marx and Engels foresaw an inevitable world war between the socialist and capitalist camps.

I propose to cite a number of the reflections of Marx and Engels, not with the intention of using them as proof of the justification of the policy of coexistence, but so one may deduce from the spirit which inspired their views through and through, how artificial an elaboration are the Chinese assertions that their criticism of the policy of coexistence is based on Marxism. If nothing else, these passages I cite show with remarkable clarity how determinedly Marx and Engels were in principle opposed to the imposition of revolution or socialism from without.

Here are a number of such reflections:

". . . the simple laws of morals and justice, which ought to govern the relations of private individuals, should be the paramount rules of the intercourse between nations.

The fight for such a foreign policy forms part of the general struggle for the emancipation of the working classes."[1]

"We opposed this playing with revolution in the most decisive fashion. In the midst of the ferment then going on in Germany to add invasion, which was to import the revolution compulsorily from outside, meant to put an obstacle in the way of revolution in Germany itself, to strengthen the government, and to deliver the legionaries themselves . . . defenceless into the hands of the German troops."[2]

"This cool estimation of the position, however, was regarded as heresy by many persons, at a time when Ledru-Rollin, Louis Blanc, Mazzini, Kossuth and, among the lesser

---

[1] Marx-Engels: *Selected Works*, International Publishers, New York, Vol. II, p. 442.
[2] Marx-Engels: *Selected Works*, International Publishers, New York, Vol. II, p. 24.

German lights, Ruge, Kinkel, Gögg and the rest of them crowded in London to form provisional governments of the future, not only for their respective fatherlands, but for the whole of Europe, and where the only thing still necessary was to obtain the requisite money from America as a loan for the revolution to realize at a moment's notice the European revolution and the various republics which went with it as a matter of course. . . It suffices to say that the reserve maintained by us was not to the mind of these people; one was supposed to enter into the game of revolution-making; we most decisively refused to do so."[1]

"But as to what social political phases these countries will then have to pass through before they likewise arrive at socialist organization, we today can only advance rather idle hypotheses. One thing alone is certain: *the victorious proletariat can force no blessings of any kind upon any foreign nation without undermining its own victory by so doing* (emphasis—E. K.). This of course does not in any way exclude wars of defence of various kinds."[2]

One could adduce many other similar thoughts. It is plain that in the works of Marx and Engels the Chinese theoreticians can find no foundation for their theory or their practice, and it would certainly be a great deal more sensible of them to accept full responsibility for the invention both of the theory and the practice.

Still less can they find a basis in Lenin, for he was unmistakably clear on this matter. He both spoke and wrote about it. Lenin's attitude is expressed in a whole series of

---

[1] Marx-Engels: *Selected Works*, International Publishers, New York, Vol. II, p. 24.
[2] Marx-Engels: *Correspondence*, International Publishers, New York, 1936, p. 399.

documents, as indeed in the practice of Soviet foreign policy from beginning to end in Lenin's time. This is very understandable, for from the very first day the young Soviet Union found those questions on the daily agenda of political practice.

Interpreting the foreign policy of the Soviet Government, Lenin takes as starting-point the circumstances which characterized the international position of the R.S.F.S.R.[1] and the relationship of forces in the world at the time. Even though the R.S.F.S.R. had at last won the position of being able to exist as an independent socialist country beside the capitalist countries, she was still constantly under the menace of direct imperialist intervention. For this reason Lenin before all else insists on those aspects of cooperation with the capitalist countries which should ensure the existence of the R.S.F.S.R. and mobilize the working class to support that cause. Urging economic cooperation and efforts to achieve peaceable agreement with the capitalist countries on any point, he attacked imperialist, interventionist circles because they were opposed to finding such agreements.

Lenin emphasized that the capitalist countries, being obliged to face the existence of the R.S.F.S.R. as an undeniable fact, were forced in their own interests to cooperate with it. He expressed his preparedness for cooperation with any country, particularly on economic matters. In this sense he even stated certain principles on which cooperation between the young socialist country and the bourgeois governments should be based (the treaty with Esthonia, the Draft Decisions of the All Russian Central Executive Committee on the Report of the Delegation to the Genoa Conference).

---

[1] Russian Soviet Federated Socialist Republic.

Lenin points out the preferability of the peaceable policy of the R.S.F.S.R. and the fact that it was precisely by that policy that the Soviet Republic had ensured its very existence. His propositions were at the same time an indirect criticism of those inside the R.S.F.S.R. itself who had expressed doubts in the appropriateness of that policy.

Here are a number of passages which indicate Lenin's views on those problems:

"Even if we have not won a victory on an international scale, an integral, solid victory, we are in such a position that we have at least won conditions in which we can coexist with the capitalist countries, which are now obliged to enter into commercial relations with us. In the process of this struggle we have won the right to independent existence."[1]

"Under reasonable conditions the granting of concessions is also desirable for ourselves, as one of the ways in which we can attract technical aid to Russia... from the more developed countries in the period in which socialist and capitalist states will coexist."[2]

"In what have we been superior to the united forces of world imperialism with regard to Esthonia, which always suffered from the forcible rule of Tsarist feudal Russia? In the fact that we have shown our ability in good time and sincerely to renounce rule by force, in order to proceed to a peaceable policy, winning the sympathy of the bourgeois government of a small state, despite the support lent this by international capital.

The development of capitalism in each country takes place at a different tempo, in a different situation, manner

---

[1] Lenin: *Works*, 4th Russian edition, Vol. XXXI, p. 384.
[2] Lenin: *Works*, 4th Russian edition, Vol. XXX, p. 21.

and method. The socialist republic of one country exists side by side with the capitalist countries of the whole world and compels their bourgeoisie to waver. Thence they drew the conclusion: 'This means that your position is hopeless; by the use of force you have defeated the White Guards, but what about all the rest of the world, what are you going to do with that?' That too we shall defeat. That this is no empty phrase the peace concluded with Esthonia is proof. All the pressure of international capital was defeated in that sphere in which our renunciation of rule by force was recognized to be sincere."[1]

". . . the peace was concluded under the conditions[2] by which we made a number of territorial concessions, concessions which did not completely correspond to strict adherence to the principle of the self-determination of nations, by which in deeds we made it manifest that the question of frontiers was a question of secondary importance to us, while the question of peaceable relationships, the question of the suitability of waiting for the development of the conditions of life within each nation, was not merely the most important question in principle, but also one of such a nature that by it we were able to win the confidence of nations which had been hostile to us. . ."[3]

". . . without certain mutual relations between us and the capitalist states we cannot have any lasting economic relations. Events very plainly show that they are also not possible for them. . .

But is it in any case at all possible for there to be such a thing as a socialist republic existing inside capitalist

[1] Ibid., pp. 294, 5.
[2] Lenin here refers to the conclusion of peace with Esthonia.
[3] Ibid., pp. 295, 6.

encirclement? It did not look feasible either in a political or a military aspect. Yet it is already proven to be possible in both a military and a political sense, it is a fact. And in regard to trade? And industrial exchanges? And links, aid, the exchange of services between backward, ruined agricultural Russia and the industrially advanced and rich group of capitalist states—is that feasible? Did they not threaten to surround us with barbed wire and say that because of this there could not possibly be any economic relations?. . ."[1]

"The most urgent, pressing and practical interests that have been sharply revealed in all the capitalist countries during the past few years call for the development, regulation and expansion of trade with Russia. Since such interests exist, we may argue, we may quarrel, we may split up and form various combinations—it is highly probable that we shall have to split up—nevertheless, after all is said and done, this fundamental economic necessity will hew a road for itself. I think we can rest assured of that. I cannot vouch for the date; I cannot vouch for success; but at this gathering we can say with a fair amount of certainty that the development of regular trade relations between the Soviet Republic and all the capitalist countries in the world is bound to continue."[2]

"We consider that completely friendly relations with both states[3] are quite feasible, and this is our aim. We consider that precisely the expansion of trade relations will inevitably have a remarkably powerful influence leading to the realization of this aim. We consider that the properly under-

[1] Lenin: *Collected Works*, 4th Russian edition, Vol. XXXIII, pp. 125-126.
[2] Lenin: *Selected Works*, Cooperative Publishers, Moscow, 1947, Vol. II, pp. 771-772.
[3] Lenin is speaking here of France and England.

stood interests of England and France will exert a like influence in this sense. We consider that the mutual interests of England and France, in so far as they come into contact with Russia, in no case contain elements of inevitable hostility between the two countries."[1]

I could adduce many other such passages, but this is unnecessary, since the Chinese authors undoubtedly know them at least as well as we do. They are also very well aware that it is quite impossible for them to offer the slightest proof that Lenin considered the policy of coexistence in principle unfeasible. On the contrary, he struggled to secure lasting coexistence. It is quite another matter that in the circumstances in which the Soviet Union was at the time he should also express a doubt whether the bourgeoisie, which at the time was still strong, would be prepared to accept the policy of coexistence. For this reason he gave a warning on the need for the world proletariat and the first socialist country to be on their guard. And it is precisely passages of that sort from Lenin's works which the Chinese theoreticians use to support their arguments. But besides this Lenin had a profound faith in the possibility of the socialist republic's holding its own within the ring of capitalist encirclement, and this meant that he had faith in the possibility of the coexistence of a socialist country and the countries of the capitalist system. In the last resort it was precisely this that was the essence of the divergences between his views and those of Trotsky regarding the building of socialism in one country alone, regarding the theory of permanent revolution and so on. All in all, it is quite clear

---

[1] Lenin: *Collected Works*, 4th Russian edition, Vol. XXXIII, p. 346.

that there is no support for the Chinese theories in Lenin's views.

Now let us look at what Lenin said about the relationship of a socialist country to war.

"Our policy and propaganda are throughout in no sense aimed at instigating the nations to make war, but to put an end to war. And experience has well shown that a socialist revolution alone constitutes the way out of eternal war. In this way our policy is not one of instigation of war."[1]

"Our experience has given us an unshakable conviction that only extraordinary attention given to the interests of the various states removes the ground for conflicts, removes mutual mistrust, removes fear of intrigue, creates that confidence, particularly in workers and peasants who speak various languages, without which peaceable relations between peoples are absolutely unfeasible, as is the satisfactory development of all that is of value in civilization today. . .

We for our part on this and allied questions would like to see as few general declarations as possible, as few solemn promises, as few elegant formulae, but as many as possible of the most ordinary, most clear decisions and steps which would genuinely lead to peace, not to speak of the complete removal of the danger of war."[2]

Concerning the imposition of any form of "making others happy" by means of war, or any sort of imposition of socialism from without, Lenin was clear and unambiguous —indeed, more so than Marx or Engels. Arguing against the authors of a certain resolution of the Moscow District Party Bureau, which at the time had been put forward in

---

[1] Lenin: *Collected Works*, 4th Russian edition, Vol. XXXI, p. 440.
[2] Lenin: *Collected Works*, 4th Russian edition, Vol. XXXII, p. 349.

opposition to the policy of the Central Committee, concerning the Brest Litowsk Peace Treaty, Lenin wrote as follows:

"Maybe the supporters of this resolution believe that the interests of the world revolution forbid making peace at all with the imperialists?... The unsoundness of this view strikes the eye. A socialist republic surrounded by imperialist powers could not exist at all, without flying to the moon.

Maybe the initiators of the resolution believe that the world revolution needs *jogging*, and that it can be jogged only by war—and in no case by peace, which might give the masses the impression that imperialism was being 'legitimatized'? Such a 'theory' would be completely at variance with Marxism, which has always been opposed to 'jogging' revolutions, which develop as the acuteness of class antagonisms that engender revolutions ripens. Such a theory would be tantamount to the view that armed uprising is a form of struggle which is indispensable under all conditions. Actually, however, the interests of the world revolution demand that the Soviet power, having overthrown the bourgeoisie in our country, should *help* that revolution, but that it should choose the *form* of help which is commensurate with its own strength."[1]

The same thought was formulated by Lenin on another occasion in considering the principle of self-determination of peoples, on which occasion he rejected the proposal that the principle of the self-determination of a "nation" should be changed to the principle of the self-determination of "the toilers":

[1] Lenin; *Selected Works*, Cooperative Publishers, Moscow, 1947, English edition, Vol. II, pp. 279-280.

"And there they influence the masses with the argument that the proletarian revolution in Germany would result in the same disorders as in Russia. Our disorders are a protracted malady. We are striving against desperate difficulties in creating the proletarian dictatorship in our country. As long as the bourgeoisie or the petty bourgeoisie or even a part of the German workers, are under the influence of this bugbear, namely: the Bolsheviks want to establish their system by force, so long will the formula 'the self-determination of the toilers' not help matters. We must arrange things so that the German social-traitors will not be able to say that the Bolsheviks are trying to impose their universal system, which, as it were, can be introduced into Berlin by Red Army bayonets. And this is what may happen if the principle of the self-determination of nations is denied."[1]

"The Polish proletarian movement is taking the same course as ours, towards the dictatorship of the proletariat, but not the same way as in Russia. And there the workers are being scared by statements to the effect that the Muscovites, the Great Russians, who have always oppressed the Poles, want to carry their Great Russian chauvinism into Poland in the guise of Communism. Communism cannot be imposed by force. When I said to one of the comrades among the Polish Communists, 'You will do it in a different way', he replied, 'No, we will do the same thing, but better than you'. To such an argument I had absolutely nothing to object. We must give them the opportunity of fulfilling a modest desire—to create a better Soviet government than

---

[1] Lenin: *Selected Works*, Cooperative Publishers, Moscow, 1947, English edition, Vol. II, p. 443.

ours. We have to reckon with the fact that things there are proceeding in a rather peculiar way, and we cannot say, 'Down with the right of nations to self-determination! We grant the right of self-determination only to the toiling masses'. This self-determination proceeds in a very complex and difficult way. It exists nowhere but in Russia, and, while foreseeing every stage of development in other countries, we must decree nothing from Moscow. That is why this proposal is unacceptable in principle."[1]

In connection with this quotation one should also add the following reflections of Lenin's:

"It is impossible to capture political power (and the attempt to capture it should not be made) until this struggle has reached a *certain* stage. This 'certain stage' *will be different* in different countries and in different circumstances; it can be correctly gauged only by thoughtful, experienced and well-informed political leaders of the proletariat in each separate country."[2]

To any objective reader, studying Lenin to grasp Lenin's views, and not to extract formal arguments for his own views from Lenin's, this would be sufficient to get his bearings. He cannot fail to reach the conclusion that not only do Lenin's views fail to confirm the propositions of the Chinese theoreticians, but some of Lenin's conclusions ring like a direct criticism of them.

Though, as they develop their critique of the policy of coexistence and their line of the inevitability of war, the Chinese theoreticians and political functionaries nevertheless

[1] Lenin: *Selected Works*, Cooperative Publishers, Moscow, 1947, Vol. II, pp. 444-445.
[2] Ibid., p. 595.

make themselves out to be the most consistent of Leninists, this does not change the objective nature of their acts.

Hence the main thing is not quotations, but the objective historical effect of any action. This effect also determines the historical role of the current Chinese criticism of the policy of coexistence. There is therefore no need for us to linger any longer on the theoretical or the ideological aspect of the Chinese propositions regarding coexistence. Instead, we will now examine those propositions through the prism of the effect they will have and in the light of the further expansion of socialism in the world.

CHAPTER 6

On the Inevitability of Armed Revolution

If the full meaning of the Chinese line of policy of the inevitability of war is to be grasped, it is necessary to examine one more theory which the Chinese theoreticians emphasize today, namely the theory of the inevitability of force, that is of armed uprising or revolutionary war in every country. This theory is also based on a group of specially selected and distortedly presented quotations from the works of the founders of Marxism and Leninism, and not on an analysis of objective data.

Here two things call for elucidation, namely, what is the point of including this theory in a discussion about peace and coexistence, and what connection has it with Marxism or Leninism?

The fact that this question has in a quite abstract form more or less forcibly been dragged into the discussions about peace and war is the clearest indication that the authors of the proposition about the inevitability of armed revolution are not interested at all in any elucidation of the matter, whether theoretical or practical, but need it solely to endow their theory about the inevitability of war with a particular sense.

In fact, this thesis, beside the thesis about the inevitability of war, is an additional foundation stone of the theory that the policy of coexistence is an untenable one. For from this thesis they draw the logical conclusion that if in more or less every country in the world the armed form of revolution and the same forms of the dictatorship of the proletariat are essential for the transition from capitalism to socialism to be accomplished, then any talk of coexistence is a reactionary act which holds up the revolution whereas war between the socialist and the capitalist world would in fact mean not only the speeding up of that development, but would itself become a form of the "world revolution". The final conclusion logically and inevitably to be drawn from such a thesis is that not only should we not struggle against war, but we should desire it, since it is precisely war that speeds up the course of the world socialist revolution.

If things are interpreted in this way, the inevitability of war is no longer—as it was in Lenin's view—the result of the fact that *imperialist contradictions* "inevitably breed wars", but becomes a reflection of the indispensability of a revolutionary settlement of accounts with capitalism. By this the Chinese theory of the inevitability of war is not merely a dogmatic repetition of old theses in new conditions, but acquires an entirely new content.

To argue the justification of their views, which deny the possibility of coexistence, and imply a wish for war to take place, they deliberately or unwittingly confuse the problem of international war with the problem of revolution and civil war. This they do clearly with the intention of proving that any war waged by the socialist countries against other countries would be in fact a revolutionary war, a sort of civil war for the extension of the revolutionary achievements, that is, a "world revolution". Here therefore we have the deeper sense of the linking of the thesis of the inevitability of armed revolution in every country with the thesis of the inevitability of war. Developed to the end, this theory would simply bring us to a justification of a specific form of modern "Bonapartism", that is, to a confusion between a war of conquest and a revolutionary war.

I will quote two passages from the writings of the Chinese authors which—despite Marxist phraseology—cannot hide their real anti-Marxist and unsocialist content:

"So long as there is counter-revolutionary force, there must also exist revolutionary force, to oppose it. It would be impossible to eliminate counter-revolutionary force without revolutionary force. Any state in which the exploiting classes are in power is counter-revolutionary force ... even when compelled not to use this new weapon (atomic bombs and rocket weapons—E. K.) an imperialist state will of course continue to be an imperialist institution based on the use of force until it is overthrown and its place is taken by a people's state, a state of the dictatorship of the proletariat of that country ... War is the most acute form of expression of rule by force. One form it takes is civil war, the other foreign war."[1]

So according to this thesis a war of conquest becomes not only the right, but also the revolutionary duty of the socialist countries, for to renounce war would be equivalent to renouncing the revolution.

Further:

"Since there exists an antagonism between imperialism and colonies, imperialism is bound to pillage and crush colonies and will inevitably incite the resistance of the

[1] *The Red Flag*, according to the *Hsinhua Agency*, Peking, April 19, 1960.

colonial peoples. Since there exists an antagonism between those who hold the reins of power, the bourgeoisie, and the people—the proletariat and broad body of a nation— the bourgeoisie is bound to make ever greater efforts to strengthen its power and will inevitably incite the revolutionary struggle of the proletariat and the broad body of the nation. Since there exists antagonism between the imperialist camp and the socialist camp, imperialism will always strive in every possible way to break up the socialist countries. Whenever unable to wage "hot war", it will certainly wage the so-called "cold war". This must prompt the socialist countries to undertake appropriate steps for self-defence. All this is independent of human will."[1]

Here again a revolutionary direction of the socialist and anti-imperialist factors inside any country is once again equated to the line of a war between the socialist and capitalist countries being inevitable.

The real political content of these Chinese theories will be still more clear if we call to memory the passage from Chang Pei's article cited above, in which he reproaches the Yugoslav communists with a revisionist attitude "particularly regarding the international class struggle".

What exactly do the Chinese theoreticians understand by the notion of "the international class struggle"? For a Marxist it can mean one thing only, the unity and mutual linking together of all the *internal* social processes throughout the world which go to make up the revolutionary transformation of the world. But to the Chinese theoreticians it in fact means the inevitability of war between the capitalist

[1] An article by Shi Tung Hsiang, in *Red Flag*, according to the *Hsinhua Agency*, April 15, 1960.

and the socialist countries. And this is, first, a flagrant distortion of the Marxist teaching about the class struggle and, secondly, justification in advance of any war which any socialist country may begin against any non-socialist country or any country which it may declare to be non-socialist.

In other words, *as soon as anybody abandons the view that the process of revolution is the process of the revolutionary resolution of internal social contradictions by the internal forces of that society, and begins to confuse international war and revolution, he is inevitably in danger of declaring one form of a war of conquest to be a form of world revolution.*

With these propositions as starting-point, the Chinese authors twist the views of the League of Communists of Yugoslavia and their Programme about the means, forms and paths of the transition from capitalism to socialism in all possible ways, in order, on the one hand, to "discover" a link between the Yugoslav policy of coexistence and reformism, and on the other to "prove" that the struggle against reformism unconditionally demands a struggle against the policy of coexistence as well. While doing this the Chinese critics try to ascribe to us all manner of views, about believing in the automatic growth of capitalism into socialism, about being in favour of a social-democratic policy of reforms as the only possible path to socialism, and so forth, whereas what the Programme of the League of Communists of Yugoslavia in fact says about this is the following:

first, revolutions are the necessary expression of the resolution of social contradictions and a need of social progress in the transition from one social system to another, but this does not mean that the revolutionary transformation and the dictatorship of the proletariat must assume the same forms, adopt the same measures, clash with the same sharpness or follow the same path of development in all countries;

secondly, it is also possible for the socialist forces in one way or another, gradually or suddenly, in a relatively peaceable way to gain political leadership and make possible the process of building up socialist relationships, and in addition such possibility of peaceable transformation is increased in proportion to the increase in the political and economic strength and the international role of the socialist countries, that is, precisely as a result of the previous achievement of other victorious revolutions;

thirdly, the growing strength of socialism and the convincing quality of its example, the steadily increasing material influence of the socialist relationships on world economic life, as also the growing awareness of people that it is impossible to go on living in the old way, powerfully speed up the process of the break-up of capitalism and prompt and compel the leading forces of capitalist society to compromises with the working-class, to concessions to the working-class. This simultaneously strengthens the positions of the working-class and makes it easier than previously for it to make use of the parliamentary means of struggle and the forms of bourgeois democracy for a gradual building up of its political influence in the community and for the gradual realization of its socialist demands and aims. And, finally, it makes it possible for much broader political forces than the communist parties to adopt the building of socialism as their programme.

85

The process of the world socialist revolution does not proceed as a war of positions waged between two fronts, but as an organic social process, in which revolutions and revolutionary and anti-colonial wars are intertwined with evolution, that is, with the processes of peaceable political struggle and the gradual acquisition of political positions by the socialist and other progressive forces, as also with material evolution on a social basis. Of course, such a path naturally calls for a great variety of political forms in the period of transition from capitalism to socialism.

Here we have always emphasized that it is primarily the internal, objective and subjective conditions of each individual country that prompt this or that path of resolution of social contradictions. It is quite certain that in highly developed countries there is greater feasibility of a more peaceable path than in less developed countries, where internal contradictions are more powerfully brought out. For this reason it is no accident that in many European countries the working-class has adopted a mainly social-democratic outlook, while in the undeveloped countries of Asia and Africa it is scarcely possible to conceive today of any appreciable social-democratic influence, whereas the influence of the communist parties is quite naturally very strong. For the same reason, for example, in pre-war Yugoslavia it was the influence of the communist party that dominated, whereas in neighbouring Austria the influence of social democracy was more powerful. Anybody who in all this tried to see merely ideological aspects of the matter, whether as accidental or transitory phenomena or solely as the reflection of subjective "characteristic features" would merely show his lack of understanding of Marxism.

On the Inevitability of Armed Revolution

Speaking of Lenin's attitude to war, here is how Krupskaia described Lenin's views on the role of the working-class in history:

"From the very outset, when he became a Marxist, he had a clear view of the tremendous role which the working-class was to play in history. In his very first articles he spoke of the great historical role which the working-class was fated to play. But at the same time, speaking of the working-class, he always spoke of one or another concrete working-class. Speaking of our Russian working-class, he would speak of what at the given moment that class alone represented."[1]

In contradistinction to that eternal, vital and creative Marxism, which though prone to error constantly checks itself by realities, the ruling Chinese Marxism of today is schematic, subjectivist and dogmatic. The opposite of Lenin, the Chinese authors examine things in a "petrified form". Hence the working-class to them is a static, unchangeable phenomenon, just like a quotation torn from its context and understood dogmatically, that is, as a pure abstraction, to which any qualities whatsoever may be ascribed, according to the views of the authors of the abstraction. Admittedly, an abstract working-class of this sort can satisfy all the requirements of the dogmatic ideological elaborations of the Chinese theoreticians and politicians regarding the strategy of the "world revolution", as a head-on clash between two systems, with a revolutionary working-class in the "enemy's rear", but this in no way corresponds to realities.

[1] N. K. Krupskaia: *About Lenin*, Moscow, 1960, p. 41.

The working-class is neither a bookish quotation nor an abstraction, but a living organism in process of development, in constant movement. Nor is it a monolithic or homogeneous whole, but a complex structure, whose features are basically determined by the most elementary fact that all workers do not have either the same conditions of labour, the same qualifications, the same conditions for the "sale" of their labour-power, the same "price" for their labour-power, or the same wages or anything else. Consequently, the reaction of the working-class and its views are also influenced by the general social and economic conditions and the actual internal set-up of the working-class. And since both the conditions and the internal set-up of the working-class change, so the concrete reactions and views of the working-class undergo modification.

Marx even in his time spoke of the phenomenon of the "bourgeoisification" of the English working-class and also of the phenomenon of a "working-class aristocracy", and Lenin of course dealt very extensively with the consequences of those phenomena. It was indeed precisely these phenomena that brought about the great split in the working-class movement.

It is quite clear that these phenomena are not solely a matter of ideological differences of opinion. Here we have material facts which have their deep social and economic roots, and they further impose a variety of forms and paths of social development leading towards socialism. This is why the Chinese theoreticians who, as the final consequence of their theories, even go so far as to admit an offensive war, that is to say, a war of conquest by the socialist camp against the camp of imperialism, are fundamentally deceiving themselves if they think that such a war will be welcomed with bouquets by the working-class in the rear of the armies of the capitalist countries. A long time ago Robespierre uttered the dictum that no people likes "armed missionaries", and subsequently Napoleon very soon found out from experience what a profound truth that was, as did everybody else who thought that the revolutionary *Marseillaise* was sufficient to subordinate Europe to the interests of the French bourgeoisie.

Here indeed we have all the profound erroneousness and harmfulness of the Chinese confusing of any modern war whatsoever with world revolution. Such a war could only rally the peoples of the whole world to the side of socialism if it were indeed a war of defence and if the socialist countries had previously done all they could to maintain peace. But a war waged according to the Chinese views could only be understood by the peoples as a war of conquest. Whoever in his policy omits making a factual analysis of all these conditions and processes which we have been discussing is very likely to find himself projecting his own illusions on to somebody else's reality and learning when it is too late how an apparently "revolutionary war" can be transformed into a war against the working-class of another nation.

Given to schematic thinking and to viewing matters in the abstract static state of some given moment, and not in their course of development, the Chinese theoreticians as starting-point take a theoretically envisageable ultimate result, formulated as the ultimate aim of the political struggle, their purpose being to "put the whole world right" in the light of that ultimate aim. This is why in their practical policy they are prone not merely to leaping over essential phases of development, but also to forcing the socialist revolution and the world into the mould of artificial, subjectivistic, theoretical elaborations. In doing this they are beginning to undermine the forces of the revolution and of socialism, egging them on to a path of adventurism in foreign policy and to the extreme consequences of a fully-developed bureaucratic *étatism* in internal policy.

The essence of revolutionary action, however, based as it is on scientific socialism, on Marxism, is not to try to create a world on the model of some ideal or other, but to liberate, to strengthen and to direct the internal forces of society which by their own action will inevitably turn that society in the direction of socialist progress and the envisaged ultimate result—which of course is merely conditional, since there is no termination to progress—in this process not building up society for any abstract ideological reasons but because their particular social-economic interests guide them in that direction.

"The social history of men is never anything but the history of their individual development, whether they are conscious of it or not. Their material relations are the basis of all their relations. These material relations are only the necessary forms in which their material and individual activity is realized."[1]

Precisely for this reason practice will never allow any man to skip over the necessary phases of development without being penalized, or to force real developments into artificial elaborations. In this respect politics is like technol-

[1] Marx-Engels: *Selected Works*, Cooperative Publishers, Moscow, 1935, Vol. I, pp. 373-374.

ogy. Inadequate means for the transmission of electric power will not only fail to give satisfactory results, but may even cause a catastrophe. Similarly, the imposition of inadequate political means and forms on any society or on any other nation cannot fail to have harmful consequences. Precisely for this reason, "making other peoples happy" by imposing Chinese or any other kind of socialism from the outside is not in the least a revolutionary aim, but on the contrary cannot but manifest itself as a reactionary phenomenon and a brake on the development of socialism.

Here we might think we had said enough, but since the Chinese theoreticians adduce Marxism and Leninism in support of their theory about the inevitability of armed revolution, we must also set these assertions of theirs side by side with the real state of affairs.

Formulating his thesis about the means to be used in the struggle for power, Marx apart from other discussions of the subject, expressed himself in the following well-known words:

"One fine day the workers must inevitably take political power into their own hands, to terminate the old sort of politics, which protects obsolete institutions, unless, like the early Christians, who regarded that task with indifference, they wish to renounce their kingdom in this world. But we have never asserted that this aim is to be attained by means that never vary.

We are aware that the institutions, character and traditions of every individual country must be taken into consideration, and we do not deny that there are countries, such as America and England—and if I were better acquainted with your institutions I might perhaps add Holland—

in which the workers may be able to attain their aims by peaceful means. But if this is so, we must also recognize that in the majority of the continental countries forcible means must be used as the crow-bar of our revolution, that it is precisely forcible means to which we must have recourse at the right moment, in order for the rule of labour to be finally installed."[1]

The Chinese theoreticians are acquainted with this proposition of Marx's and themselves refer to it, but— with unjustified reference to Lenin too—they declare that conditions have changed and that in fact things are no longer the same as they were when Marx wrote. For that matter, in theory they do allow for a "peaceful" transition to socialism, but in the realities of today they consider this unfeasible.

That conditions have changed is certain. In our view they have changed, not in the direction of lessening, but of increasing the possibility of attaining the aims of the socialist revolution by relatively peaceful means. But even were the opposite to take place, even if events did in fact deny the rightness of Marx's words, still the Chinese theoreticians would not be able to refer to Marx for support when they deny the possibility of reaching the aims of the working-class by peaceful means, for in fact they justify their attitude precisely by rejecting Marx's proposition.

On the same subject, Engels wrote the following:

"It may be presupposed that the old society might develop peacefully into the new in countries in which a people's government holds all power in its hands, where

---

[1] Marx: *Speech at a Meeting in Amsterdam after the Hague Congress, The First Second and Third International.* Published by *Rad*, 1952, pp. 121, 122.

provided one has the majority of the nation behind one, it is possible to do whatever one wants—in such democratic republics as France and America and in monarchies such as England . . ."[1]

As these words show, Engels did not even shrink from the clear formulation: "the old society might develop peacefully into the new". Fortunately, he was in no danger of dogmatic minds giving him a bad mark because he used words which were "taboo". To any man who grasps the spirit of Marxism it is obvious that by saying this Engels had not "lapsed" into reformism, but was defending Marxism. He of course in this connection never for a moment had in mind an automatic, elemental growth of capitalism into socialism, but a process of struggle of the working-class for the leading social role, for power, in which by relatively peaceful means of political struggle the working-class *step by step solved the tasks of the socialist revolution.* In essence he said just the same as Marx.

Lenin of course also accepted Marx's and Engels' attitude on this question. I have already quoted Lenin's views which show that in principle he did not differ from Marx even on this matter, and I will not repeat those words here.

Nevertheless, in Lenin's day the question did not arise whether in the struggle for power, in addition to forcible methods, peaceful methods too were feasible, but *vice versa,* whether the proletariat should adopt forcible methods at all. At this time Lenin was obliged to struggle against reformism, which in principle denied forcible methods as a weapon of the proletariat in the struggle for socialism. He

[1] Marx-Engels: *Works, Soviet Party Publishing House* of the Central Committee of the All-Union Communist Party (Bolsheviks), 1936, Vol. XVI, p. 108.

was obliged all over again to fight to establish the ideo-logical confirmation of Marx's theses about revolution by force and the dictatorship of the proletariat. And this was necessary not only for theoretical, but still more for practical reasons: revolution was knocking at the door, and the working-class parties had to make it their aim, had to make ready for it and be prepared to organize and realize it. It should be clear to anyone that in such a situation Lenin had no reason whatsoever to prove the theoretical pos-sibility of the use of peaceful means in the struggle for socialism, but in the given conditions had every reason to emphasize the indispensability of revolution by force.

And now, from the fact that at this precise juncture Lenin considered that there was "less possibility" of a peaceful transition to socialism than in Marx's day, the Chinese theoreticians conclude that it is anti-Leninist to speak of the feasibility of "peaceful means" in the process of the socialist revolution, and that consequently the Pro-gramme of the League of Communists of Yugoslavia is on this question reformist, opportunist, revisionist.

However, it was precisely Lenin who wrote the following words about this kind of "Marxism":

"Our teaching, said Engels referring to himself and his famous friend, is not a dogma, but a guide to action. This classical proposition emphasizes with remarkable force and expressiveness that aspect of Marxism which is continually left out of view. And in leaving it out of view, we turn Marxism into something one-sided, crippled, and dead, we take from it its living soul, we undermine its fundamental theoretical basis—dialectics, the teaching of historical de-velopment as being all-sided and full of contradictions; we cut its connection with the definite tasks of the epoch, *which may change* with every new turn in history."[1] (emphasis E. K.).

Consequently, the Chinese theoreticians have no right whatsoever to refer to Lenin in defence of their dogmatic theses. This they themselves know very well. This is why some of them on every possible occasion make the point that Lenin allowed for peaceable development solely "as an exception". For that matter, even this claim of theirs is not accurate, but in this context that is not important. What does matter here is whether peaceable development is or is not feasible. If it is, whether rarely or frequently, the historical process itself will determine the course of events. That it is feasible only the realities of history prove, not the quotations I have adduced, and not only the realities of the socialist revolution, but those of all the revolutions in the history of mankind. No revolution was ever repeated in the same form in another country. Every revolution differs from every other, and the victory of a revolution in this or that country has always been accompanied by changes effected through the more peaceable forms of all sorts of political crises in other countries, in the end bringing about a similar social transformation. But it is also quite certain that without the great revolutions there would also not be these small social changes or peaceful forms of social transformation.

Consequently, we do not differ from the classics of Marxism on this matter, except in so far as differences arise from the varied nature of the conditions in which we live and

[1] Lenin: *Marx, Engels, Marxism*, International Publishers, New York, 1935, English edition, p. 85.

those in which the authors of the classics of Marxism and Leninism lived. But the differences between the Chinese concepts and the classics of Marxism and Leninism are important, they are differences of principle.

For that matter, from the standpoint of the present-day circumstances of the struggle this hypertrophied discussion about the nature of the means of revolution is out of place, and would indeed be incomprehensible, were it not that behind it is concealed an intention of interpreting the theory of the inevitability of war in a special way. In the last resort, the process of the development of the socialist revolution in the course of more than forty years has proved both the necessity of revolutionary methods of force and the indispensability of struggle by peaceable means. What is more, in the world of today circumstances which are quite contradictory are being created. For instance, in certain countries the communist parties can be isolated, squeezed out altogether as a political or historical factor, unless they are able to make use of peaceable methods of struggle, while in other countries the communist parties will come to the same fate unless they are able to make use of the conditions of a revolutionary situation and overthrow the rule of force of the reactionaries by methods of force. For that matter, experience yields instances of both cases. In circumstances of relatively peaceable social development empty revolutionary phraseology isolates communists, so that they prove incapable of establishing themselves as a leading factor when it comes to conditions of revolutionary sharpening of the internal social contradictions, whereas in fact things should be precisely the other way round, that

96

is, *the means of struggle should not be fixed by rigid dogmas but determined according to the concrete objective and subjective circumstances of the struggle at the moment in question.* For, as Engels said:

"... any means that leads to the aim suits me as a revolutionary, whether it is the most violent or that which appears to be the most peaceable."[1]

These are the clear words of a Marxist, and of any revolutionary realist, concerning the means of struggle.

But clearly the Chinese theoreticians are not concerned with clarity in this matter, but with an argument in favour of something else, namely, the following thesis: if the possibility of the victory of socialism by peaceable means does not in practice exist in the remotest corner of the globe, it is all the easier to prove that coexistence is an illusion, a self-delusion, and that war can also be a weapon of the world revolution. The ultimate consequence of this argument is that whoever is "afraid" of war, that is, who is for coexistence, is against the revolutionary struggle for socialism and in favour of reformism.

[1] Engels: *Letter to Herson Trier of* 1889, *Second International*, published by *Rad*. 2nd edition, 1952, p. 102.

CHAPTER 7

On Just and Unjust War

Yet another theory plays a fairly large part in the Chinese criticism of Yugoslav foreign policy and the policy of co-existence as such, namely, a theory about just and unjust war. It is only when we subject that theory too to examination that we obtain a complete picture of the Chinese idea of a socialist international policy for our time.

The meaning of this theory, as explained by the Chinese theoreticians, might be defined in the following way: since wars are divided into just and unjust wars, communists are not against all wars, they are only against unjust wars, and if a war is just, they cannot be against it, for that would be to compromise with evil, with imperialism, it would be opportunism, withdrawal from a revolutionary position. Thus here we have logic stood on its head.

For the ultimate consequence and simultaneously the explanation of this thesis would be that since as the ineluctable form of resolution of contradictions in the "international class struggle" war between the world of capitalism and the world of socialism is inevitable and is also from the standpoint of socialism just and revolutionary, one should not struggle against it. What is more, to struggle against it is in the spirit of this logic just as wrong as it would be to struggle against the revolution in any country.

To all these arguments, of course, is tied a string of accusations and slanders against the communists of Yugoslavia, such as that they make no distinction between just and unjust war, that "like all pacifists" they are against any war and that this means entering into a pact with imperialism, refusing aid to oppressed peoples who are struggling for independence, and so on.

I have no intention of spending time on these accusations and slanders. It is well enough known that socialist Yugoslavia has within the limits of her capabilities always offered the oppressed peoples consistent all-round support in their struggle for liberation as she has all other progressive and anti-imperialist movements. Certainly no slander whatsoever can conceal that fact from the nations which are struggling and in their struggle feel the support of Yugoslavia. As far as this goes, these Chinese critics too are well aware of it. For this reason their slanders merely serve to reveal how uneasy they are, how displeased, because of the good name which the consistently progressive, democratic and anti-imperialist policy of socialist Yugoslavia enjoys precisely among the peoples who are fighting for their independence—and that uneasiness points to the weak points not of Yugoslavia's policy, but China's.

A little more needs to be said in this connection about the meaning of the Chinese spokesmen's own interpretation of the theory of just and unjust wars.

By this formula Marxists at an earlier stage tried to define what attitude the working-class should assume regarding the wars of their own nation, or of their bourgeoisie, that is to say, when the working-class should support a war and when it should struggle against it. They considered that the working-class should support national, defensive, liberational and revolutionary wars, but should oppose any war of conquest and particularly imperialist wars aimed at the division of the world. The first they defined as just wars and the latter as unjust wars, not with the idea of giving any absolute scientific or political evaluation, for this terminology is not appropriate to such evaluations, but solely in order to indicate what political action the working-class should engage in regarding one or the other sort of war.

In this sense this formula even today, given the same circumstances, is still up-to-date and has the same significance. In conformity with it we supported Egypt during the attack on Suez, we support the national liberational war of the Algerian people, we opposed the intervention in the Lebanon and so on. Similarly we shall also continue to offer all possible support to any nation which is engaged in a just war for its national liberty and independence from aggressors or imperialist conquerors.

If we now place the theory about just and unjust wars, understood in this way, side by side with the Chinese interpretation of the theory, we are struck by two contradictory points in these two interpretations.

First of all, it is clear—from all that we have outlined above—that the Marxist theory about just and unjust wars refers solely to an evaluation of the character of any war and of the relationship of the working-class to any war which has broken out independently of the working-class or has been forced on it, and that it cannot possibly mean that the working-class should be for any war or should even fight in any war which may be just. Precisely the classics of Marxism and Leninism have always emphasized that it is not the mere justness of a war that should determine the attitude of the revolutionary proletariat to it, but the part that war plays in the whole complex of international developments. Even very just wars can have a reactionary effect. For this reason, Lenin considered that it would be wrong to support a war, however just in itself, if that war were to cause reactionary repercussions on a world scale. As an instance Lenin picked out precisely the war between Serbia and Austro-Hungary. Similarly Lenin in principle condemned wars about frontiers, for all that they might seem to be just, for he considered that here was another question which should be tackled by internal struggle and not by war, which would do more harm than good. Speaking generally, the classics of Marxism and Leninism, with their profound faith in the internal social processes of each country considered that reliance should also be placed primarily on those processes in the attempts to solve questions in dispute between nations. All the more did they reject as absurd the mere thought of an international war for such a cause as the spreading of socialism.

This becomes particularly clear if we examine the matter through the prism of the relationship of the social forces in the world today. The war we are discussing, the only war possible today—apart from local wars and national-liberation wars—is a world war between the bloc of the socialist and the bloc of the capitalist countries. This means that the situation has fundamentally changed since Marx's and Lenin's day. Today beside the capitalist states there are also socialist states, with their armies. their military technology, their economic strength. The contradictions are concentrated between these two great camps. Here the question is not whether war between these two camps would be just or not, but whether the leading socialist forces should adopt the line of trying to resolve those contradictions by war or by other means, that is, by internal social processes. *This means that the concrete problem is not whether the socialist countries and forces will or will not support a war which breaks out independently of them or is forced on them, but whether they should themselves make the decision whether war is or is not indispensable for the resolution of the existing contradictions, whether they are to pursue a policy of war or a policy of peace and coexistence.* There is only one solution to this dilemma which is in conformity with Marxism and the humanistic spirit of socialism: if there are any ways of resolving those contradictions other than war, the socialist forces can and should pursue solely a policy of peace and coexistence. We all know not only that there are such other ways of solving the contradictions, but also that war as such simply is not an instrument capable of resolving contradictions of this sort.

However, in the eyes of the Chinese critics the Yugoslav communists are "American agents" and they "put a fine face on imperialism" precisely because in this dilemma they are for peace and coexistence, that is to say, struggle against war. So the formula about just and unjust war as interpreted by the Chinese turns into a peculiar mystification, the sense of which is that you may not fight for peace if any war which interrupts peace is a just war. As we have already seen, such a conclusion would be correct only if war were the sole means of tackling the solution of a specific contradiction. Here is the Achilles' heel of the Chinese theories. Thus the anti-Yugoslav slanders of the Chinese critics are no proof at all of the wrongness of the Yugoslav policy, while at the same time they throw a strange light precisely on the Chinese concepts of the socialist revolution in the world of today as a war between "the east and the west wind."

Thus the logic of the Chinese theoreticians is not very convincing, but its political result is more than clear.

But this is only one aspect of the Chinese application of the formula about just and unjust wars, and as it happens, a less important aspect. The most important thing here is the question of what in the Chinese interpretation is a just war. If we leave aside certain accurate evaluations of colonial and revolutionary wars, the attitude of the Chinese theoreticians boils down to a theory that a just war is any war waged by a socialist country, because socialism is progressive and capitalism is reactionary. Here in fact the theory of just and unjust wars is brought to the ridiculous conclusion that any war which *I* wage is a just war.

However, if we put things in this way, the question of whether or not war is just loses any meaning whatsoever. Namely, if we have in mind a defensive war, it is out of place to attack the Yugoslavs, for in Yugoslavia there is really not a man who would not consider that socialism must defend itself if attacked. If however it is a question of whether the socialist countries should strive for such a world war, once again the question of justness or unjustness is not evaluated from the standpoint of which is the more progressive, socialism or capitalism, but from the standpoint of the real consequences of such a war for the peoples of the world, for the fate of socialism and social progress. Here in advance we must declare that such a war is in principle contrary to the interests of socialism and not even the Chinese interpretation of the theory about just and unjust wars can change anything here. I shall return to this point again later.

When we take together all the Chinese theories which we have discussed and through which the Yugoslav policy of peaceable and active coexistence is criticized, we get the following chain of argument: coexistence is untenable, since war is inevitable as the form which the revolutionary resolution of contradictions in the "international class struggle" takes, while war in itself is just, so it is wrong to disseminate any illusions about peace and coexistence, but we should set a course for war, in which we would be the stronger, a war in which the sacrifices would "be redeemed" and which would terminate in the victory of socialism in the whole world.

I do not mean by this to assert that the Chinese critics of the policy of coexistence consciously and openly favour war. On the contrary, they too declare that they are against war, and latterly have even been allowing a certain possibility of the "imperialists being forced to accept peace", which in the last resort might be a sort of line of retreat for the Chinese theoreticians. However, the matter does not lie in the words but in the logic of the Chinese concepts, which in the last resort identify world war with the class struggle, with revolution. And the moment this identification is made, the line that war is inevitable becomes the necessary conclusion for practical politics. But now this line again of itself becomes a source of fresh erroneous conclusions: the policy of coexistence becomes an illusory policy, even a reactionary one. In other words, the moment somebody considers a war in which he himself will be one of the main protagonists to be inevitable, he simultaneously begins to prepare and instigate that war, whether he so intends or not.

It is in complete opposition to the spirit of Marxism to take the fact that a war is waged by a socialist country as the sole criterion of the "justness" of that war. In the last resort, it is not merely a matter of whether a war in the name of socialism, against capitalist countries, can under certain conditions—objectively, against the will of the socialist countries—turn out to be a war with the working-class of those countries, which will defend its own bourgeoisie in the name of national independence. What matters is that such a war might impose more backward political forms of socialism in much more developed social-economic circumstances, and in this way play a reactionary role. It is also possible that such a war would encourage unsocialist trends, such as hegemonism and similar phenomena. And, finally, it is not difficult to deny the existence of socialism in another country and then "in the name of socialism" to declare "just" any pressure on that country, to the point of war itself against it.

Is such a possibility merely a theoretical supposition? No, we have a very recent example of it—the pressure on socialist Yugoslavia. All the Chinese theoreticians without exception—in one form or another—deny the socialist character of Yugoslavia, and this, in the spirit of the logic of the Chinese views of the moment, means that they are declaring Yugoslavia to be an "outlaw" country. There is an old Yugoslav proverb deriving from Ottoman Turkish times which says "The Kadi[1] accuses and the Kadi judges".

[1] The Turkish judge.

Precisely for this reason, today even more than in the past, those principles of Marx, Engels and Lenin by which they fundamentally condemned and rejected any policy aimed at the imposition of socialism or of one or another set of socialist relationships from outside, by war, should be cherished. That attitude on the one hand makes for a realistic appraisal of the immediate harmful social-political consequences of the responsibility which the socialist forces would assume if they adopted war as an instrument for the imposition of socialism, and on the other hand just as realistic an understanding that no socialist country merely by being socialist automatically becomes immune to egoistic aims or acts. Everybody knows that distortions, errors and the emergence of all manner of negative trends not only go with the development of a young society on the road to socialism, but may also appear in the foreign policy of a socialist country, especially in the relations between the nations in the period during which neither narrow-minded nationalism nor great-state hegemonism are quite dead. Precisely for this reason the classics of Marxism never excluded the possibility of a socialist country also waging *an unjust war*. Practice confirms that such phenomena are not quite out of the question.

Lenin, who was both as scientist and revolutionary realist well aware that in the matters of hegemony and war socialist states too might make mistakes, succumbing to their own narrow egoistic interests, wrote the following on the matter:

"Engels by no means considered that the economic factor would by itself, directly, settle all difficulties. The economic transformation will prompt *all* nations *to move*

106

towards socialism, but in this process revolutions against the socialist state and wars are also feasible. Politics will inevitably conform gradually to the economic set-up, but that will not happen all at once and will not come about smoothly, or simply, or directly. As unquestionable Engels insists solely on one unconditionally internationalist principle which he applies to all 'alien peoples', that is to say, not only to the colonial peoples: forcing happiness on them means undermining the victory of the proletariat.

The proletariat will not be sacrosanct or proof against errors or weaknesses merely by reason of having brought about a social revolution. But eventual errors (and selfish interests—efforts to ride on others' backs) will inevitably bring it to a realization of this truth."[1]

Having this in mind, apart from other factors, Lenin always opposed easy estimates based on the solidarity of the world working-class, and wrote:

"... it is absolutely absurd to declare that we must conceal every concrete difficulty of our revolution today and say: 'I stake everything on the international socialist movement—I can commit any piece of folly I please'."[2]

How in the light of this, we may ask ourselves, should a world war in present conditions be evaluated? Everybody knows that such a war would not only last a long time, but would be frightfully destructive. It is not hard to see all the possible egoistic trends which in such circumstances, borne on the wings of power, might come to the surface in the name of socialism. Even if it were a war of defence, it would strike hard blows at the development of socialism,

[1] Lenin: *Works*, 4th Russian edition, Vol. XXII, p. 337.
[2] Lenin: *Selected Works*, International Publishers, New York, Vol. II, p. 291.

for a long time to come twisting certain sectors of social and international relations out of shape, not to speak of what would follow were the war the result of such a policy as that which some of the Chinese article-writers suggest.

Perhaps, under the influence of local conditions, the Chinese theoreticians think that a world war under the conditions of their country would not have such destructive consequences as people say, but might even assist the country to free itself from economic backwardness. But is it possible for the other socialist countries to accept this logic, least of all those which would have to assume the main burden of the war and the main blows of modern military technique? Can the peoples of the socialist countries assume the responsibility for the terrible sacrifices and the destruction merely in order by means of total war to "make others happy" by the imposition of their social system? Clearly, not only can they not do so, but the working people of the socialist countries would never give their support to an adventurist policy leading to such an aim.

Consequently, what is in question is not merely the justness of war according to the Chinese criteria, but a whole series of other factors which determine or should determine socialist policy regarding war. Considering this matter in all its complexity, we are of the opinion that at the present day one of the central tasks of the socialist forces and at the same time one of the most powerful ways of furthering socialism is precisely to strive for peace and for peaceful, active coexistence, that is, to strive to have world contradictions resolved not by war but by internal social development. This development will at the same time exert its influence in the sense of a gradual modification of international relationships on new foundations, in harmony with the spirit of peace, equality and cooperation among the nations, that is, with that spirit which socialism or rather, socialist principles of democracy and humanism, should gradually bring into those relations.

CHAPTER 8

The Old within the New

Even though the Chinese theories discussed in this study are in their actual political content in a certain sense a new phenomenon, produced by the Chinese Revolution, in their ideological form they are not quite new. Internal contradictions similar to those characteristic of present-day Chinese society gave rise to similar theories in the first period after the October Revolution.

I have no intention of asserting that the ruling theory of the Chinese communists is Trotskyist, but yet the extraordinary similarity which does exist between the two theories once again is convincing evidence that like circumstances breed like ideologies.

Trotsky did not believe in the possibility of the maintenance, or rather development of socialism in the Soviet Union unless the revolution were extended to Western Europe. To a mind so superficial, static and so given to abstract schemes as Trotsky's it was impossible to accept the fact that before them stood a long-drawn-out day-to-day struggle, full of hardships, against tremendous difficulties, both in the internal and in the foreign policy of the young Soviet republic.

And indeed those difficulties were exceptionally great. The new Soviet state was being built up in circumstances of great economic backwardness, with a numerically very small working-class and with a very limited number of skilled cadres loyal to the revolution, with very extensive breeding-centres of counter-revolution, and with a heavy ballast of conservatism in the mentality of a large part of the nation. The internal sources of economic advancement were relatively very weak and undeveloped and indicated that there would be an arduous and relatively slow development of the economic foundations, certainly much slower than the hopes which had inspired the revolution had counted on. The world which surrounded the first socialist state was a hostile one, firmly determined to liquidate it at the first opportunity, and powerful enough to make such threats real. That it was unable to realize those threats at once, in the first years of the revolution, was above all the merit of the world working-class, which tied its hands. But it had never renounced that aim, and indeed made every effort by economic and political blockade to drown the revolution in its own difficulties and contradictions. In addition, not only did the hopes of a European revolution not materialize, but it became clear that it would be necessary to face the fact that before the first socialist country stood a long period of isolated existence as an island surrounded by the ocean of a hostile world.

To Trotsky this seemed a completely blind alley, a total defeat of the world revolution, the Russian Revolution being the last unit of that world revolution, now encircled, which must either break out of the encirclement or die gloriously. This outlook resulted in his putting his hopes in an adventure, which would have been condemned in advance to failure, namely, war. His theories of permanent revolution, his arguing about the impossibility of building up socialism in the isolated Soviet Union, his dogmatic forecasts of the inevitability of a war of united imperialism against the Soviet Union, his faulty assessment of the internal factors of social development in other countries, all expressed in an unrealistic expectation—which for that matter was so cruelly shown to be false outside Warsaw in 1920—that the European proletariat would at the first step taken by the Red Army automatically rise against its own bourgeoisie—all this was a reflection of the psychotic state into which Trotsky had fallen in his blind alley.

For that matter, quite apart from this, Trotsky's whole mental outlook was one of simple expectation of elemental revolutionary impulses, for he was incapable of perceiving the social factors which prepare and drive revolutionary impulses, or of distinguishing the paths or the means by which conscious revolutionary socialist thought can influence the movement and strength of such factors. He saw the revolution as a fact in isolation, that is, as an abstract historical inevitability, and could not see it as something interconnected with a multitude of other forms of social movement, or as something that had to be prepared by the internal development of every country. Precisely for this reason he thought the Russian Revolution was in a blind alley just when, on the contrary, it was on the threshold of a victory in the field of world history.

In contradistinction to Trotsky, Lenin saw all these phenomena from a different angle. Whereas to Trotsky the defeat of the European revolution was the blind alley of the Russian Revolution, to Lenin it was merely a signal for a change of political tactics. The defeat of the European revolution was not absolute. Though it had not succeeded in handing power to the working-class, it had succeeded in preventing the European bourgeoisie from making any effective intervention in the Soviet Union. Further, it had produced a number of other advantageous results, which had strengthened the social-political part played by the working-class. To Lenin this meant not merely the feasibility of avoiding war for a considerable time, but also, at least theoretically, the possibility of avoiding war altogether. There therefore was the prospect not merely of building up socialism in the Soviet Union, but also of economic cooperation between the Soviet state and the capitalist world which would facilitate and speed up the building of the foundations of industrialization in the U.S.S.R. The strengthening of the working-class movement, its revolutionary victories in certain countries, the further expansion of the national liberation movements in the colonies, internal changes in the capitalist world—all this could not but gradually improve, never worsen, the situation of the first socialist country in the world. The fact that the Soviet Union did maintain its position despite intervention during the several years of the civil war was for it a victory of significance in world history and at the same time yet another proof of the feasibility of building socialism in one country. Indeed, it is precisely in the integral nature, the interconnectedness, interweaving and all the mutual impacts of all those processes and contradictions that we have the true process of the world socialist revolution, not a "victorious march" of the Red Army through Europe, but a never-ceasing process of internal social developments in every country and their interconnecting on the international, world-wide scale.

With those views as basis, Lenin in both theory and practice stood opposed to the theory of permanent world revolution, which as formulated by Trotsky had lost its Marxist character and had been transformed into the ideological programme of a policy of war adventure, calling for the European communist parties to adopt a sectarian and conspiratorial policy. Counter to this he drew up a new policy for the Soviet state, one based on a lengthy period of coexistence of the states of the capitalist system and those of the socialist system, a policy, that is, of peace and peaceable coexistence and of economic and other cooperation with the capitalist countries. With this, Lenin considered that the socialist state should offer whatever support to the progressive and revolutionary movements and forces in other countries was in the given circumstances feasible, provided it did not threaten the existence of socialism and the socialist state.

Criticism of Lenin's thesis of the feasibility of the victory of socialism in a single country was for Trotsky merely his starting-point and an argument for his basic theory, that of permanent world revolution, which in the last resort would have boiled down to a war of the Soviet Union against the capitalist world, in the hope that it would start a revolution in Western Europe and the world as a whole. One should add that Trotsky did not clearly formulate this consequence of his theory, but by the internal logic of his theory this follows automatically.

History has relegated Trotsky's theses to oblivion, for experience has shown them to be completely false. Yet the vital elements of those theories now reappear on the world stage in the Chinese theories.

114

The Old within the New

In 1928, criticizing the programme of the Third International, Trotsky wrote:

"The unshakable conviction that the fundamental class aim... cannot be realized by national means or within national boundaries, constitutes the very heart of revolutionary internationalism. If, however, the ultimate aim is realizable within national boundaries through the efforts of a national proletariat, then the backbone of internationalism has been broken. The theory of the possibility of realizing socialism in one country destroys the inner connection between the patriotism of the victorious proletariat and the defeatism of the proletariat of the bourgeois countries."[1]

"If we take into consideration onlyt he economic lever, it is clear that we in the U.S.S.R., and all the more so in China and India, have a far shorter arm of the lever than world capitalism. But the entire question is resolved by the *revolutionary struggle* of the two systems on a world scale."[2]

These passages in the first place show how abstractly schematical and subjective Trotsky's thought was in its very nature. He starts from an "unshakable conviction", then with one stroke of the pen he abolishes nations and their role in the social development of our time, as if mankind had already reached a stage in developing the forces of production which eliminated the social-economic role of nations.

Further, these passages go to confirm what I have already emphasized earlier, that criticism of the thesis concerning the possibility of building socialism in one country

[1] L. Trotsky: *The Third International after Lenin*, New York, 1936, p. 72.
[2] Ibid., p. 211.

115

was, as an expression of the capitulation of Trotsky's dogmatic spirit when faced with the realities of an economically backward country, merely the springboard for his theory of permanent world revolution. If we take the first quotation—that is, the denial of national equality and independence—together with the second—that is, with the proclamation of world revolution as a way out of the economic backwardness of the U.S.S.R.—it is not difficult to grasp the real material content of the tendency which inspires the two theories. Obviously, that tendency could only be born in circumstances of an arduous struggle against backwardness, and this from the conviction that only the overthrowing of the bourgeoisie in the developed countries by revolution or war could bring the Soviet Union not merely final victory but also the economic means with which to overcome its internal economic and social-political difficulties and contradictions.

For the same reasons Trotsky, just like the Chinese theoreticians today, condemned any policy of coexistence, considering it to be a form of manoeuvre and thereby automatically self-delusion.

In the same work he wrote:

"The contradiction between the U.S.S.R. and the capitalist world is a fundamental one. There is no escape from it by way of manoeuvres. By means of clear and candidly acknowledged concessions to capital, and by utilizing the contradictions between its various sections, the breathing spell can be extended and time gained, but even this, only under certain historical conditions, and by no means under any and all circumstances. It is gross self-deception to believe that the international bourgeoisie can be "neutralized" until

116

the construction of socialism, that is, that the fundamental contradictions can be overcome with the aid of a manoeuvre. Such self-deception may cost the Soviet republic its head. Only the international proletarian revolution can liberate us from the fundamental contradiction."[1]

Behind this pseudo-radical language is concealed not merely the basing of policy on the inevitability of war, but also a desire to see it come to war, as the way out of the internal contradictions of the Soviet society. "If the revolution does not prevent a war," Trotsky wrote on another occasion, "war will be able to help the revolution", and thereby gave a complete interpretation of his theories. This argument too, of course, bears a striking likeness to certain arguments of the Chinese theoreticians.

Unlike Trotsky, the Chinese theoreticians do not say anything about the impossibility of building socialism in a single country. After so much experience, that today would be completely unconvincing. However, what is important is not the theory but its sources and its conclusions in the field of practical politics, and these are the same in the case of the Chinese theoreticians as in Trotsky. This can easily be grasped from all that the leading Chinese functionaries and journalists write and say about the questions of war and peace. *In fact, what criticism of the thesis concerning the possibility of the building of socialism in a single country was to Trotsky, criticism of the feasibility of peaceful coexistence is to the Chinese theoreticians.*

In general, it must be emphasized that the theory of the possibility of building socialism in one country did not play the part in Lenin's views which later Stalin and Trotsky

[1] Ibid., p. 137.

117

ascribed to it. To Lenin the essence of the question was not whether it was possible in one country to realize the "final aim" of the socialist revolution—for Lenin's mind was too profoundly scientific to venture into such static predictions—but whether a victorious country of the socialist revolution could continue to exist when encircled by capitalism, could it proceed to the building of socialism and the development of socialist social relationships, could it defend itself against the possible aggression of imperialism or could it prevent such aggression altogether? Lenin's answer to all these questions was a positive one, coupled with all the necessary warnings as to the quality of imperialism, which by its very nature remained a source of wars and the menace which these constituted for the first country of socialism. In other words, the essence of the theory of the possibility of building socialism in one country is precisely the thesis concerning the possibility of coexistence of countries of differing social systems, that is, a thesis about the indispensability of building one's plans, as Lenin himself said, on "a lengthy period of coexistence".

By these very arguments Lenin rejected war between the Soviet Union and the capitalist world as an instrument of Soviet policy in extending the world revolution, which was the ultimate consequence of Trotsky's views. Convinced of the impossibility of imposing the revolution from without, Lenin vigorously opposed any illusions about that "victorious march" of the revolution into Western Europe, and instead turned his attention to internal socialist construction and to peaceful coexistence with other countries. Thereby all along the line he opposed those leanings towards foolhardy Bonapartist adventure which as a final consequence arose from Trotsky's arguments. For indeed any attempt by war to impose one's own overlordship in the name of the socialist social system would in fact be only a modern form of Bonapartism.

One hundred and sixty years ago, many European revolutionaries welcomed Napoleon as the bearer of the French Revolution into feudal Europe, in the hope that this way, without any great trouble, they too would achieve the revolution. That illusion cost them dearly. Only a few years later they had become either outcasts of their nations, which were struggling to achieve independence, or allies of their own feudal reactionaries, engaged in a struggle for national independence against Napoleon. But even Napoleon broke his neck in this effort.

"The general war against Napoleon was the return blow of the national sentiment of all the nations which Napoleon had trampled underfoot."[1]

It has become obvious that nobody can conduct an aggressive war in the name of revolution and go unpunished.

Trotsky forgot those lessons of history, or else he thought they did not hold for the socialist revolution. But nevertheless there they were, and they have been confirmed in various ways in the most recent stages of history. It would seem as if the Chinese theoreticians of today are also sometimes forgetful of those lessons, since they so lightly equate world war and socialist revolution. And when they make this erroneous prediction they are not only at fault in respect of socialism in general but also in respect of the elementary interests of their own revolution, for all they thereby achieve is to cut it off from other progressive forces.

[1] F. Engels: *Rule by Force and Economics of the Creation of a New German State.*

It would of course be out of place and mistaken to make a mechanical comparison between two periods. Socialism in itself constitutes the negation of any Bonapartism. But that does not mean that in the transitional period there can be no appearance in the name of socialism and revolution of what Lenin described as "selfish interests and attempts to ride on somebody else's shoulders", whether it is a question of the defence of economic privileges previously acquired or the employment of political force in order to overcome one's own economic weakness. Either can yield only reactionary results. Either may be the source of deformations of socialist international policy which as an historical phenomenon can, *mutatis mutandis*, be compared with the phenomenon of Bonapartism at the beginning of the nineteenth century.

In the Soviet Union Lenin put an ideological end to such tendencies and this set the course of the development of the Soviet Union in all respects—and not only of the Soviet Union. Only so great a mind as Lenin's was able to rise above the empiricism and pressure of the concrete, material realities of the situation in which the October Revolution was placed and perceive the prospects of that revolution from the standpoint of the general, historical interests of socialism. This is why he was able in this direction also to seek and to find solutions to concrete problems of the Soviet Union. This tremendous ideological achievement of Lenin's also had its influence on Stalin's period. It can be said that in spite of occasional waverings and inconsistencies in which he came very close to the views of Trotsky, nevertheless in the last resort Stalin in this question did stick to Lenin's way of seeing things. It is certainly to his merit that the Soviet Union did not succumb to pseudo-radical adventurist tendencies which would have made it the easy prey of imperialism. It was precisely the policy of coexistence—based on the theory of the feasibility of building socialism in one country—which despite his inconsistencies and waverings Stalin nevertheless did in practice implement, that ensured not only the existence but also the economic expansion of the Soviet Union.

However, all this does not mean that these particular tendencies of egoistic "armed messianism" cannot appear elsewhere and in other circumstances. Today there is no "pure" socialism, free of all egoism and the vestiges of old outlooks, so such phenomena cannot be excluded. This makes it all the more necessary for the conscious socialist forces to oppose any "theory" which tends to justify such phenomena. And there is no question but that the policy of coexistence plays just the same role and helps restrain such tendencies as the theory of the possibility of building socialism in a single country did in Lenin's day.

I have discussed this stage—historically now a past stage—of ideological contradictions of socialism at some length to make it easier for us to compare the present-day conflicts of this sort with those already past. Anybody who is in the least familiar with the development of the first stages of the October Revolution must be struck—despite the differences in terminology—by the extraordinary similarity of the views set out in the Chinese literature and speeches and the views of Trotsky.

I repeat, by this I do not mean to assert that the Chinese communists are ideological disciples of Trotsky. But it is obvious that like historical circumstances produce like ideological developments, as the reaction of men to those circumstances. In the first case those developments suffered crushing defeat, in the second they have in one country received temporary status—but that is no proof that they are any more "Marxist" today than they were at the time of the October Revolution. On the contrary, it merely shows to what extent Chinese Marxism has been made really Chinese, that is, subjected to revision or "modification" according to the needs of the day-to-day policy and practice of China at the present moment.

Of course socialism gains from the extension of socialist practice in the world, but Marxism very often "loses", since it is subordinated to the immediate practical demands of everyday life, for in the minds—or, to be more precise, in the hands—of certain people concerned with political theory and practice it often undergoes very strange metamorphoses. Lenin for that matter envisaged such a fate for Marxism. On one occasion he wrote:

"The international revolutionary movement of the proletariat does not and cannot proceed evenly and in the same form in different countries. Thorough and all-sided utilization of all possibilities in all spheres of activity comes only as a result of the class struggle of the workers of various countries. Every country contributes its own valuable original traits to the general stream, but in every individual country the movement suffers from some kind of one-sidedness, from some theoretical or practical shortcoming in the individual Socialist Parties."[1]

[1] Lenin: *Selected Works*, Cooperative Publishers, Moscow, 1953, English edition, Vol. IV, pp. 302-303.

It would look as if this prognostication of Lenin's, after being confirmed in other countries, is now once again being confirmed in China too.

True, we need not worry our heads much about that realization in itself. For those who are not dogmatists, socialism is not something which retains the same form forever, something which is constructed according to some ready-made "Marxistic" formula, but is a historical process, developed by millions of people by reason of their normal work, a process which must inevitably give birth not only to new forms in practice but also to new ideological set-ups. Those who act in such varied objective circumstances are inevitably under the influence of those circumstances, and the more they are given to empiricism, the more does this come to expression. And any practice tends towards empiricism. Of course, under such conditions Marxism too goes through a process of evolution—here in one, there in another direction. For of course, socialism nevertheless does develop, does expand, does go forward, and with it its science too.

In this sense we too would not be disturbed merely by the existence of a Chinese variety of Marxism, or even by the quite un-Marxist claims that anybody is the only true interpreter of "true Marxism" such as the leading circles of the Chinese Communist Party put forward today. What is disturbing is the material essence of those theories, that is to say, the fact that elements of the old policy, of the old system and methods, which have no connection at all with socialism, are imposed on others in the name of "true Marxism", and with all the force of political pressure. For this is a trend which points to a grave appearance of hegemonistic tendencies. Such deformations in the development of socialism in our day must be resisted by progressive socialist thought, and this not in the name of any other "true Marxism", but in the name of that historical progression which is the only cause that Marxism can serve, in the name of democratic relations between the socialist countries and all peoples, in the name of the principles without which socialism becomes merely an empty word.

For that matter, it would seem that we are not the only ones to have noticed the similarity between the Chinese views of today and Trotsky's views, for the present-day successors of Trotsky have themselves already noticed it.

For instance, in the Trotskyite magazine *The Fourth International* we can read the following:

"The Chinese views stood in sharp distinction to the honeysweet official Russian statements on the possibilities of peaceful coexistence. Revolutionary Marxists can only welcome this distinction, favourable to the Chinese Communist leadership."[1]

The article then goes on to criticize certain views of the Chinese leadership as inconsistent, but above all the Chinese leadership is criticized for not assuming a completely consistent attitude as to the inevitability of a new world war. Quoting a passage published in the *Red Flag*[2], to the effect that the Chinese communists are for peace and against war, but that they are not afraid of war, the commentary goes on to reproduce the following reflections:

"If they are taken *as such*, every revolutionary could only applaud these words, insofar as their meaning is a

1 *4th International*, Spring 1960, No. 9, p. 39—original text.
2 An article published on April 1st in *Red Flag* under the heading *Imperialism as the source of war in modern times and concerning the path of all the nations in the struggle for peace.*

revolutionary one. But at the same time they have an *anti-revolutionary* aspect, are contradictory, like the whole policy of the Chinese Communist Party. They correspond to similar, though less courageous, *routine* statements from the Soviet bureaucracy, which have the tendency to threaten the imperialists with the consequences of a war, in order to make them accept peaceful coexistence."[1]

After giving a general appraisal of the article in the *Red Flag*, and comparing it with the Soviet attitude regarding questions of war and peace, the authors of the commentary conclude:

"No doubt the *Red Flag's* article is... a great step forward. Only sectarians could neglect this positive side of the Chinese attitude towards imperialism. It reveals at the same time... that China is orientating towards a more revolutionary policy *on a world scale*. This can only be welcomed by every revolutionary Marxist."[2]

Consequently, the Trotskyites of today agree with the Chinese policy in so far as it rejects the policy of coexistence and proclaims the inevitability of war as a form of the world revolution. On the other hand, they reproach it with not being sufficiently consistent and decisive, that is, for not going on to say "B" after saying "A". In other words, having once declared the inevitability of war as a form of the world revolution, they should at once go on to make a further declaration in favour of such a war, that is, should not merely threaten war, but actually make war. Thus the Trotskyites exercise direct pressure in favour of the acceptance of a Bonapartist war as a weapon of socialist

---

[1] Ibid., p. 43—original text.
[2] Ibid., p. 43—original text.

policy in which they have certainly surpassed even Trotsky himself, who in that respect avoided committing himself.

However, the "error" of our modern Trotskyites in this case consists merely in the fact that they follow the political logic which otherwise lies at the foundation of Trotsky's policy and of the trends of present-day Chinese policy to the point of absurdity. Indeed, "A" is followed by "B" in every proper ABC. In other words, if you think war is advantageous, you ought to be in favour of war.

But this also means the following: *an unreal appraisal of the circumstances which exist of necessity also leads to unreal conclusions and to the application of inappropriate means, and hence to crushing defeat. Whoever assesses the circumstances of a war badly, suffers defeat; and from defeats which are the consequence of error even socialism cannot save you, just as Napoleon could not be saved by the tricolour of the French Revolution.*

CHAPTER 9

The Sense of Peaceful and Active Coexistence

It is not only we in Yugoslavia who support peaceful coexistence of nations with differing social systems, other socialist countries do so too. This policy, one might say, is even the official policy of the socialist camp. And not only is it the official policy, it also corresponds to the most elementary interests of the peoples of the socialist countries, hence in all these countries it enjoys tremendous popular support. Because of this, the force does not exist in those countries which could change that policy. For all these reasons it is not easy for the Chinese critics to attack this policy directly. So they have resorted to doing so indirectly, that is, to attacking the Yugoslav policy of coexistence in such a way that it appears as if this policy of coexistence were different from that which Lenin supported and which today the other socialist countries support.

However, the manoeuvre has been so clumsily performed that one might almost think its protagonists really wanted everybody to grasp what it was all about. I will quote a number of statements of leaders of the three great communist parties, statements with which the Yugoslav communists not only agree, but which they actively support in everyday practical application. Were the Chinese theoreticians too to agree with them, they obviously would not feel any need to engage in polemics about the Yugoslav concepts of coexistence. Not that I would say that in the practical implementation of this policy there are not certain differences, but it is nevertheless plain that there are no differences of principle between the Yugoslav views and the views of the authors of the statements which I will now adduce.

Here are the quotations, without comment, since they speak for themselves:

"We assert that in our day the real possibility of excluding war from the life of society finally and for all time is already being achieved. This possibility derives from the new relationship of the international forces created after the Second World War."[1]

"Peaceful coexistence... is not a tactical move but a basic principle of Soviet policy.

If we say that in the rivalry between the two systems— the capitalist and the socialist—the socialist system will win, this by no means signifies that victory will be achieved by armed intervention of the socialist countries in the internal affairs of the capitalist countries.

The policy of peaceful coexistence is gaining ever broader international recognition... This is consistent with the laws of things, for in present-day circumstances no other way out is feasible. In fact, there are only two ways—either peaceful coexistence, or the most destructive war in history. There is no third way."[2]

"The socialist countries do not in the least fight against war and for peaceful coexistence because capitalism is still

---

[1] N. S. Khrushchev: *Speech at the National University of Indonesia, Gadja Mada,* Pravda, February 22, 1960.
[2] N. S. Khrushchev: *Report to the XXth Congress of the Communist Party o the U.S.S.R.*

strong. No! We simply do not want any more wars. Even so noble and advanced a system as socialism cannot be imposed by force of arms, if a people does not want it. For this reason the socialist countries, pursuing a consistently peaceful policy, concentrate their efforts on peaceful construction and by the force of example in the building up of socialism warm the hearts of men and lead them. The question when this or that country will take the road of socialism will be decided by the people themselves. This for us is the most sacred thing we know."[1]

"What does the peaceable coexistence of the capitalist and socialist countries mean? It means mutual respect for each other's territorial integrity and sovereignty, non-aggression, non-interference in internal affairs, for economic, political or ideological reasons, equality and mutual advantage, coexistence. The principles of peaceful coexistence have already met with broad international recognition."[2]

"Supporting the policy of peaceful coexistence of states with differing social structure, we of course have no intention of asserting that there are no contradictions between socialism and capitalism, that complete harmony can be established between them, that there can be any peace concluded between the communist and the bourgeois ideologies. Anybody who adopted such a view would have abandoned Marxism-Leninism. The ideological differences of opinion are irreconcilable and will continue to exist, but this does

[1] N. S. Khrushchev: *Speech delivered when welcomed in Peking on the occasion of the Tenth Anniversary of the People's Republic of China.* September 30, 1959.
[2] N. S. Khrushchev: *Speech at a meeting in Moscow dedicated to Soviet-Czechoslovak friendship,* July 12, 1958.

not exclude peaceful coexistence and peaceful competition between the socialist and the capitalist countries."[1]

"Once again the communists declare that they have never egged anybody on to use forcible methods of rule and will never do so. Besides, the very notion of a revolution imposed by foreign armies is absurd and ridiculous."[2]

"A third world war would mean no less than the prospect of the end of human civilization such as we know it today, the civilization of which we are proud, i.e., would mean the prospect of transforming the main centres of this civilization, above all in Europe, into a chilly graveyard."[3]

"In short, what is required is the pursuance of a new European and world policy based on the abandoning of the military blocs which divide the world and drive it on to war . . .

The period of the cold war now past culminated in such changes in the world situation that any country interested solely in a policy of peace, which is anxious to implement such a policy, is in no danger whatsoever of being isolated or at the mercy of any hostile bloc. The world has become polycentric. Even in the heart of the camp of the imperialist powers there are differences which can serve as the basis for a national policy of peace."[4]

"We asserted with decision: 'No, war is not inevitable'. This problem was in its essence thoroughly thrashed out by the XXth Congress of the Communist Party of the Soviet

[1] N. S. Khrushchev: *Speech at a jubilee sitting of the Supreme Soviet*, November 6, 1957.
[2] *Points for a policy declaration of the Communist Party of Italy at the VIIIth Congress, Kultura*, 1957, p. 111.
[3] P. Togliatti: *Report at the Plenum of the Central Committee of the Communist Party of Italy* on December 9, 1957.
[4] P. Togliatti: *Report to the VIIIth Congress of the Communist Party of Italy.*

Union. This Congress emphasized the difference between the economic and the political aspects of this question. So long as there is imperialism, there will also be the economic basis which makes feasible the instigation of a war. But war is not only an economic phenomenon. When we ask whether it will come to war or not, the relationship of political forces, the conscious will of men and the degree to which they are organized together all play a great part. Today there are sufficient forces for such a catastrophe to be prevented."[1]

Even Stalin, who for reasons of internal politics often adopted very contradictory attitudes about certain of the matters we are discussing here, so in many points was very close to the present-day Chinese views, nevertheless regarding support for peace and coexistence never lapsed into the adventurism to which the Chinese communists are so prone.

When asked on September 17th, 1946, by the *Sunday Times'* correspondent, Alexander Werth, whether the further development of the U.S.S.R. towards communism did not reduce the possibilities of peaceful coexistence, Stalin replied:

"... I do not doubt not only that the possibilities of peaceful cooperation will not be reduced, but that they may even be increased ..."

In an interview with Elliot Roosevelt on December 21st, 1946, first published in the American magazine *Look*, when asked whether he thought peaceful coexistence between the U.S.A. and the U.S.S.R., including refraining from interference in each other's internal political affairs, was feasible, Stalin replied:

[1] M. Thorez: *Report to the XIVth Congress of the Communist Party of France*

"Yes, of course it is. It is not only feasible, it is sensible and completely realizable. At a time of maximum tension in the war period, differences in forms of government did not prevent our two countries' joining forces and conquering our enemies. The maintenance of such relations in time of peace is still more feasible."

Consequently, it is not we with our policy of coexistence but the Chinese theoreticians with their theses about the inevitability of war who have no backing, neither in the classics of Marxism and Leninism, nor in the present-day views of the communist parties, nor even in Stalin, to whom they refer so much.

The "fortunate" circumstance which enables the Chinese theoreticians to distinguish "revisionist" coexistence from "non-revisionist", is the fact that we call our policy one of *active* coexistence.

That word "active" becomes the subject of all manner of empty phrases about the revisionist nature of the Yugoslav concepts of coexistence, as distinct from the "true" or "correct" policy of coexistence. In passing it may be remarked that the Chinese critics have also been joined by certain other critics of Yugoslav foreign policy in certain other socialist countries, as if they would like to assure both themselves and the world that the Chinese critics are right when they attack the Yugoslav policy of coexistence and do not attack theirs.

Now let us look more closely and see what this word means which in the writings of the Chinese critics has suddenly acquired such magic revisionist power that it has turned coexistence into something that is not "true coexistence".

The Sense of Peaceful and Active Coexistence

The coexistence of states with various social systems is first of all nothing new, or anything which needs to be invented or argued out. It already exists. For forty years now two different social systems have been living side by side, and in the Second World War the first socialist country even fought in a coalition of some capitalist countries against other capitalist countries, positive enough evidence of the coexistence of differing systems being a powerful historical reality, capable of lasting over a lengthy historical period and also a great world war. This reality, even the Chinese authors admit, for forty years of history cannot just be wiped out. What is more, the very notion of coexistence is not in any way a socialist invention, nor was it only born with Marxism, since the whole of history is in fact an eternal coexistence of various social systems, for the simple reason that society is incessantly developing and changing and the wars which have interrupted coexistence were not a reflection of the untenability of coexistence but the internal law of development of all forms of class society.

What is new is the fact that in the present age we have the phenomenon of a socialist society which cannot develop to the full if war and the contradictions between the nations in general are not eliminated from the world, but are merely changed for others, as has already happened before in history. The forces of this young socialist society have already grown so that they are capable of exerting a vital influence on the development of the whole world today. And this means that in all probability they are already capable of preventing war, that is, would be capable of preventing the interruption of coexistence, were they to strive to do so. In other words, *in essence the socialist policy of coexistence is nothing else but a policy directed at the prevention of the interruption of coexistence by war.*

This and nothing else is the sense of the Yugoslav policy of coexistence.

Of course, the policy of coexistence is not and should not be a policy of defence of the *status quo*, neither in international relations nor, still less, in internal social relationships. It simply means renunciation of war as a means of resolving international contradictions, and basing oneself at the same time on the results of internal social development, which in the last resort will also change international relationships.

However, at the same time coexistence itself becomes a factor which prompts and accelerates all these processes. Since socialism has become not only a political force but also a powerful international economic force, it is plain that this force that socialism exerts, this role it plays, will influence and should indeed influence not only the over-all development of international relationships in the sense of consolidating peace among the peoples, but should also speed up all revolutionary, democratic and generally progressive processes in the social life of all nations. Only peoples liberated from the threat of a world war will give their whole attention to tackling their own social problems.

And not only this. The ever more powerful phenomenon of a socialist world in international relations influences and will increasingly influence the course of events by the introduction of new democratic and socialist factors into international relationships, factors such as mutual respect among the nations and democratic relations between them, all-round cooperation and *rapprochement*, cultural ties, the advance-

134

ment of world industry and the international division of
labour, the elimination of economic exploitation in international economic relations, the organizing of aid to the
insufficiently developed countries, the setting up of appropriate organizations and services to ensure international cooperation and an international division of labour, the setting
up of the necessary international conditions for peaceful
competition in the sphere of the productivity of labour
and of the practical checking of the effectiveness of social
institutions and relations through the results which all nations
and all men experience.

All this, of course, cannot but influence internal developments in the various countries, both capitalist and socialist,
in the sense of strengthening the socialist, democratic and
anti-imperialist forces in them.

In this way, in conditions of coexistence, the socialist
countries and all the socialist forces become a most powerful
factor in changing the world as it exists. This active role
which the socialist and all progressive and peace-loving
forces should have in the circumstances of coexistence at
the present day is the first reason why we often call our
policy a policy of *active* peaceful coexistence.

It is however not the only reason. It is clear that coexistence between two blocs which are closed and armed to
the teeth cannot be the foundation of a lasting or stable
peace. In fact, such coexistence is today already a fact,
but it is a fact with which the world of our time does
not feel either very satisfied or very sure. The problem lies
in the fact that a further step is required, that is, peace
and coexistence need to be consolidated by a striving for
disarmament, for collective security, for the elimination of

economic discrimination, for the strengthening of the all-round cooperation of states, and so forth. We have always been of the opinion that the policy of coexistence inevitably demands a stubborn struggle for the gradual overcoming of the barriers between blocs, by as intensive as possible an international bilateral and multilateral cooperation of peoples of various social systems. Consequently, for peace to become more stable we need to strive for the world to be not the coexistence of armed blocs, but the coexistence of nations which will all work together intensively in all fields where there are common interests. In other words, stable coexistence is possible solely on the basis of active and all-round international cooperation. In the final result, of course, coexistence and peace will be all the sounder, the more active are all those material and subjective factors of social progress in the world of today that multiply the forms of cooperation and inter-linking of the peoples of the whole world, and in this way increasingly tend to bind together their interests within the framework of world economy and the world-wide development of the productive forces.

Here is how Comrade Tito has defined this aim:

"Coexistence should be understood not in the sense of peoples and states merely dragging out their lives side by side, but as international relations on completely new principles, appropriate to our age, such as may make possible the liveliest peaceable activity between states even when these have differing social systems. The precondition for such coexistence is that all questions in dispute should be settled in a peaceable way, and the use of force and war ruled out. It does not mean merely a temporary lull or

manoeuvre, in the sense of each trying to outsmart the
other during such a lull. It means more lasting standards
and principles, which in our age should dominate in international relations. Coexistence excludes any interference in the
internal matters of other nations. We must never confuse
the principles of coexistence in international relations with
the internal development in any country, with social changes,
with the development of society or the relations between
the classes. It is for the peoples of the various states each
to decide in what direction and by what path the development
of the internal social system in their countries is to go.
Then, by just such a stern application of the principle of
coexistence between states and peoples as this, and by
non-interference in the internal questions of others, will
a more peaceful and painless process of social changes be
made possible in the various countries."[1]

Here we thus have yet another explanation of why we
so frequently speak of *active* coexistence. But as far as that
goes, if anybody dislikes that word *active*, he need not worry,
he may leave it out. That will not change anything in our
policy of coexistence.

Of course, one should not be under any illusion. In this
struggle the forces of socialism, progress and peace will
meet with powerful resistance from the imperialist forces
and other reactionary elements of the capitalist system, which
will strive not merely to maintain their own privileges, but
to extend these. However, it is not solely a matter of what
these reactionary forces would like to achieve, but rather
of what they are capable of achieving. *If the socialist forces*

---

[1] Tito: *Report to the Vth Congress of the Socialist Alliance of the Working People
of Yugoslavia*, April 18, 1960, *Fifth Congress of the S.A.W.P.Y.*, Kultura, p. 54.

*have a jot of faith in themselves and in the future fruits of
socialism, they must also have faith in the force of the
influence which, by reason of its peaceful and active international policy, socialism will have on the total development of
mankind today.* Precisely by a policy of coexistence and
peace and only by such a policy can the socialist forces
play their part as the representative of the basic interests
of all nations, and find support in every country. These
are, so to speak, the "everyday demands" of international
politics. The struggle for the realization of those demands
cannot but rally the forces of all advanced mankind in its
struggle against all forms of oppression and exploitation.
As it transforms its internal social relationships the world
will be ever more capable of transforming the international
relationships of the world as well.

It is indeed strange logic to assert that imperialism is
a "paper tiger" and at the same time to declare that the
vast and powerful socialist world is incapable of forcing
that "paper tiger" to maintain peace except by means of war!

The policy of coexistence is simultaneously the only way
which makes it possible for the socialist countries not only
to achieve rapid material development, but also to speed up
the development of social and political relationships towards
the higher socialist forms. Material backwardness in the past
and the arduous political conditions in which the development of the socialist countries has taken place, have hampered and slowed down the development of socialist relationships, which is why conservative thought has often prevailed
and acted as a brake on social advancement. To get free
from that brake is the great task of the socialist world.
The socialist countries can only "win" the world by example,

and not by menace and the threat of war. *This is precisely why their internal advancement becomes the principal task of the present age.* That however is a task which cannot be achieved otherwise than in conditions of peace.

CHAPTER 10

What Is Revolutionary and What Is Not

The basic line of argument of the Chinese theoreticians in this matter of war or peace is the assertion that a line based on coexistence means a line based on "class peace" and on the reformist view of the road to socialism. To prove the correctness of their attitude in this respect, they first turn the sense of the policy of coexistence for which Yugoslavia consistently fights inside-out, then go on to discuss what is really their own invention.

Here is what they say:

"The aim of the modern revisionists is to introduce confusion into the peaceful foreign policy of the socialist countries . . . Thus they consider that peaceful coexistence of countries with different social systems means that capitalism can grow peacefully into socialism, that the peoples in the countries ruled by the bourgeoisie can renounce the class struggle and pursue 'peaceful cooperation' with the bourgeoisie and imperialists, and that the proletariat and all the exploited classes should forget the fact that they live in a class society and so on . . .

All these arguments of the Yugoslav revisionists are intended to poison the minds of the proletariat and the peoples of all countries and assist the imperialist policy of war."[1]

---

[1] *The Red Flag*, according to the *Hsinhua Agency* bulletin of April 19, 1960

What Is Revolutionary and What Is Not

On another occasion another author dots the 'i's' of these arguments:

"Everybody knows that the struggle between the oppressed and the oppressor is a life-and-death struggle, in which one or the other must win. World peace and peaceful coexistence between countries with various social systems can be helped only by waging resolute struggles against imperialist oppression."[1]

We have already emphasized that, striving for peaceful coexistence, the Yugoslav communists are not only not against the "class struggle" or against the struggle of "oppressed against oppressor", just as they are not for "peaceful cooperation" of the working-class and the bourgeoisie, or of the oppressed peoples and the imperialist overlords, but on the contrary consider that in the conditions of coexistence all those forms of struggle will develop more intensively than in a period of cold war and fear of a new world war. Consequently the Chinese interpretation of our views on the policy of coexistence is from beginning to end a crude forgery and blatant slander.

However, our explanations are certainly not going to convince the Chinese critics of the rightness of Yugoslav policy. But it is held—and we are of that opinion too—that practice is the best test of the correctness of a theory. So let us have a look at what practice has to say about the revolutionary effect of the Chinese theories and the revolutionary effect of the policy of coexistence. A certain amount of experience in this direction has been already accumulated, although there has not been much time for testing.

[1] *Speech of Lui Ning Yi*, President of the Chinese Trade Unions, at a session of the General Council of the World Trade Union Federation in Peking, according to the *Hsinhua Agency* bulletin, June 8, 1960.

Socialism and War

In the post-war development of international relations mankind has—if we leave aside the first post-war years—gone through two phases: the phase of the cold war and the phase of a relative relaxation of tension, that is, of a measure of establishment of the policy of coexistence. What from the standpoint of socialism and social progress have these two phases given us?

The cold war phase, and the policy of intimidation connected with it, produced the Atlantic Pact, the closing of ranks of the non-socialist world, the greatest degree of isolation of the socialist camp since the war, the restoration of German militarism, pressure on socialist Yugoslavia, a tendency of the internal difficulties of certain socialist countries to increase, the forcing of internal social problems in the capitalist world into the background under the pressure of the atmosphere of war danger, and the weakening of the communist and other revolutionary movements in a number of countries—in a word, a number of setbacks.

On the other hand, in the phase of a decrease of tension, however slight and inconsistent this has been, there have been a number of significant events. In a few years the colonial system has suffered decisive blows—it had been undermined and smitten with decay earlier, but to some extent had been still held together by the atmosphere of the cold war. In a number of countries important revolutionary and other progressive changes have taken place. The strongpoints and sources of imperialist strength have been markedly reduced. The number of members of the UNO has grown and thereby conditions within that organization have improved and the influence of the uncommitted countries has increased. The forces of peace and coexistence in

Western Europe and America have grown stronger, including here certain circles of leading statesmen. The possibilities of unity of the working-class movement have increased, or at least the standing of all parts of this has been improved. Opposition to the policy of force has been strengthened, as also has the aspiration of the peoples for an independent and active role in the struggle for peace, independently of bloc allegiances. Such extreme reactionary products of the cold war as developed in South Korea and elsewhere have begun to fail and the notion of coexistence and a policy of non-alignment is seizing hold of broad masses of the people and is producing action in such countries as Japan. In South America revolutionary democracy has won a series of victories. In Western Europe resistance to the restoration of German militarism has begun to grow stronger and aspirations for peaceable cooperation with the U.S.S.R. and other socialist countries, including China, are also growing firmer. People are increasingly turning their eyes to internal problems of social development, which gives new stimulus to the socialist and all progressive forces and undertakings. In other words, in a very few years of a relative easing of tension and partial establishment of the policy of coexistence, the forces of socialism, of social progress in general and of peace have grown stronger, while the forces of war have been checked and weakened.

Or to be still more concrete: whereas the policy of coexistence in the sense given here has tended to disarm the forces of war and of extreme imperialist reaction, the Chinese policy of exacerbating things has everywhere, especially in the Asian countries, been sowing doubts of the peaceful intentions of the socialist countries, frightening people away from communism and objectively strengthening the forces of reaction and the protagonists of military blocs, as if deliberately striving to dig a deep gulf all down the line between the socialist camp on the one side and all the other countries of the world on the other. The peoples cannot understand it when the great Chinese state exacerbates relations with its peaceable neighbours over small frontier questions, just as they cannot grasp why in the name of socialism and revolution it defends in other countries the established Chinese capitalists' and traders' positions which in their own country the Chinese liquidate. It is no wonder that such a policy is interpreted as a great-power policy and that this arouses mistrust and even fear. One needs only to recall Lenin's policy regarding neighbouring countries to see how little justification the Chinese theoreticians have to refer to Leninism in defence of what they do.

If we assess the revolutionary quality of a policy by its results and not by a false verbal radicalism, it is certainly not difficult to answer the question, which of these two policies is revolutionary and which, whether anybody so intends or not, objectively serves precisely the war-mongers and those circles in the capitalist countries which stand for a policy of force in present-day relations between East and West.

Of course, in defending themselves against such arguments, the Chinese leaders draw attention to the events in Japan and South Korea as confirmation of their policy. On the contrary, however, precisely those events in Asia speak out most eloquently against the Chinese concepts. Objectively, the Chinese policy has supported Syngman Rhee in Korea and the most reactionary circles in Japan. The

Japanese people rose up against the linking of Japan with one of the blocs just because it was in favour of peace and because it saw its future in the policy of coexistence. And it rose up precisely at the moment when the policy of peaceful coexistence had begun at last to show results.

All this once again goes to confirm that pseudo-revolutionary ultra-left radicalism produces the same reactionary results as does open capitulation to the forces of reaction.

The same sectarian and ultra-leftist features and comparable negative results are also shown by certain Chinese tactical approaches to other immediate problems of socialist policy and international relations.

Let us, for instance, take the problem of the undeveloped countries. While the conviction is increasingly growing in the world that one of the corner-stones of the policy of peace and progress—and also of the struggle for socialism as a world system—is a narrowing of the deep gap between the economically developed and undeveloped countries, the Chinese authors today anathematize any action in that direction.

Thus the President of the All-Chinese Federation of Trade Unions, Lui Nin Yi, at a session of the General Council of the World Federation of Trade Unions, in Peking in June 1960 came out in open opposition to the aspirations of the peoples of the newly created states to speed up the development of their countries by foreign economic aid and, proclaming such aspirations to be revisionism, made the following statement:

"The so-called 'aid' of imperialism to the undeveloped countries is in fact 'an export of capital', and the aim of this is to 'intensify aggression, exploitation and control over the recipient countries' in order to seize maximum profits and aid the bourgeoisie, 'not at all to bring happiness to the people of these countries'. No organization which genuinely represents the interests of the working-class dare allow imperialist 'aid' to be confused with the sincere and friendly assistance which the socialist countries offer without any conditions."[1]

Liu Chang Sheng, Vice-President of the World Trade Union Federation, added the following to this thesis:

"It is said that after disarmament imperialism will use funds earmarked for war purposes for the 'well-being of the toiling masses' and for 'offering aid to the insufficiently developed countries', as also that it will 'contribute to the general advancement of the world as a whole without any exception'. This is indeed to put a fine face on imperialism and conceal its nature and this certainly aids imperialism, led by the United States of America, to trick the peoples of the whole world."[2]

First we here need to clear up two matters of principle.

First, the President of the Chinese Trade Unions has clearly purposely confused the "export of capital" in the classical imperialist form with organized international aid to the undeveloped countries, for which—together with other nations—we too stand. It is at least as clear to us as it is to him that the essence of imperialism is not the wish to give assistance but to subordinate another country economically. But what we assert is *that the relationship of forces in the world, and in connection with this also the*

---

[1] According to the *Hsinhua Agency*, June 7, 1960.
[2] According to the *Hsinhua Agency*, June 8, 1960.

consciousness of mankind and the relations between the peoples, have so changed that it becomes practical politics to strive for a democratic international organization for economic aid to the economically insufficiently developed parts of the world. It goes without saying that the capitalist monopolist organizations resist such trends and will continue to do so, but this is far from saying that for this reason one should stop striving for that aim. Demands of that sort fall *into the category of that "struggle for everyday demands" in international politics which mobilizes the peoples in the struggle for independence and economic advancement and narrows down the material and political basis of imperialism,* and with it those classical forms of the export of private capital which become the source of the extraction of super-profit from the economically undeveloped countries.

In the last resort the point is, what is the function of the capital invested in the national economy of a country, whether it contributes to the development of the internal productive forces or has the role of plundering those forces in the interests of the export of super-profit for the pockets of the foreign owners of the capital.

The aid for which we are striving is of course not a characteristic of capitalist relationships. But in the world of today it is not solely capitalist relationships and capitalist forces which rule, but also socialist forces and relationships as well. Striving consistently and stubbornly for an organized international democratic system of economic aid to the undeveloped countries, and at the same time against any form of exploitation or politically conditioned "aid", the socialist forces will in fact merely offer support to the elementary aspirations of peoples living in underdeveloped countries to free themselves from economic dependence. For this reason the struggle for such an aim becomes practical politics and has already given definite results. Apart from this, experience *shows that today's political relationships have brought even the capitalist countries* to the position of being obliged to make certain concessions to the principle of aid. I do not assert that this is tantamount to achieving socialism in international relations, but it is a result which shows how practical and necessary it is to strive for organized international aid to the undeveloped countries.

On the other hand, it is China that has reduced even normal trade relations with Yugoslavia to a minimum, merely in order to exert political pressure on her, and this is yet another proof—after the one which in his time Stalin offered by the economic blockade of Yugoslavia—that in the relations between socialist countries too a great deal still remains to be done, for economic aid really to be both always and lastingly unselfish and unconditional.

And secondly, in official Chinese speeches and articles, as an argument against international aid to the undeveloped countries, there is also the assertion that such aid will assist only the bourgeoisie of the undeveloped countries and consolidate its position. And this, clearly on the principle "the worse, the better", is said to be definitely not good for the revolution.

Nowhere can all the anti-scientific, cramped and static dogmatism of the Chinese theoreticians be seen so clearly as in this very example. These theories of theirs see the world as motionless every part. Capitalism is bad, hence aid to the undeveloped countries for economic development is harmful, if capitalist relationships rule in them. Therefore, a revolutionary should be against the economic development of the undeveloped countries.

If this theory is accurate, Marx was profoundly in error when he wrote about the great progressive role of capitalism in the first stages of its development. Although they declare themselves to be infallible defenders of the dialectic, the Chinese theoreticians are completely unable to grasp that a process can at the same time be both one thing and the other, that is, that in it there can be something which should be supported and something which should be rejected and criticized, and that the first should be supported precisely so that the criticism would acquire scientific and political force.

Naturally, if any capital whatsoever—from socialist or from capitalist countries, with or without conditions—is invested in the economy of an undeveloped country in which capitalist relationships dominate, the role of that capital will be of the same nature as the role of capital generally in the capitalist system, that is, it will create, or reproduce, capitalist relationships, and together with them also a class struggle between the bourgeoisie and the working-class.

However, can the Chinese theoreticians conceive of a class struggle or struggle for socialism without a working-class?

The first condition of a truly socialist, that is, working-class movement is the existence of a modern working-class, that is, of a certain level of industrial development. And this in the circumstances of today is attained in two ways, either by the classical development of capitalism or of a national bourgeoisie and working-class, or by means of state-capitalist forms and relationships, which in certain conditions can become either the starting-point for socialist development—if the subjective factor which ensures such a development exists—or the starting-point for the formation of a national bourgeoisie.

However, in all three cases economic development constitutes a historically progressive fact and facilitates, not hampers, the struggle for socialism. In all three cases, on the one hand the economic prerequisites of socialism are strengthened, and on the other, the working-class and its social role is strengthened, not to speak of the principle of national independence, which in certain circumstances and with an appropriate policy of the socialist forces can also be a factor making for a considerable narrowing down of the material basis of imperialism, which the experience of a number of non-aligned countries goes to show.

All this holds even if nothing changes in the social relationships of the undeveloped countries. However, economic aid may even have a direct influence on the development of those relationships, in the direction of strengthening the economic and social-political prerequisites of socialism, even indeed socialist development itself.

In the world of today we come upon all sorts of state-capitalist relationships, all differing one from another in their forms and in their social-historical roles. While in the developed countries such relationships grow out of monopolies and assume the aspect of state-monopolistic capitalism, which strives in new ways to preserve the essence of capitalist relationships, at the same time in many a more backward country the state-capitalist forms appear as the expression of the progressive role of the state in its efforts to speed up the economic development of the country. It depends on the internal political grouping of political forces whether such forms are merely a transitory stage on the path to the formation of a national bourgeoisie and capitalism or whether they will become the lever for a direct transition to socialism. The prime movers of such developments at the present time, now that socialism has become the dominant factor of the age, are not always only the communist parties, but in greater or lesser degree also other anti-imperialist movements. For this reason, the economic strengthening of such tendencies may also mean a direct stimulus to socialist enterprise in certain countries. In the last resort, all the socialist countries have also passed and are passing in greater or lesser degree through state-capitalist forms.

It would be narrow-minded and impotent sectarianism to proclaim that it would be better for world socialism for the undeveloped countries to remain undeveloped, so that they would be more revolutionary. That would be the same as being against the struggle of the working-class for higher wages, in order to make it more revolutionary. Above all would it be detrimental to international socialism if the socialist forces did not see the possibilities of specific forms of socialist development in such countries.

Of course, I do not think here that things are likely to develop towards socialism by elemental processes. But for this very reason—other things apart—it is necessary for the socialist countries to have a quite definite attitude in regard to aid to the economically undeveloped countries.

There is no room in the framework of this essay for any detailed discussion of this aspect of the matter, but it is quite clear that today the socialist forces cannot and should not renounce economic means which might speed up social progress—in conformity with their material possibilities—wherever possible.

Without a working-class there can be no socialism or advance at all. Consequently, to sit with folded arms and watch the economic development of backward countries, while repeating the sectarian catch-phrase "the worse, the better", means nothing else but leaving it to others, that is, to imperialist and reactionary social forces in their own way to become the leading factor in the economic life and the social development of the undeveloped countries.

Is it perhaps for tactical reasons, that is, so as not to come into conflict with the mood of the masses, that the Chinese politicians are against striving for economic aid to the undeveloped countries? On the contrary, if they shared the attitude which some Chinese communists advocate, the socialist forces would dig a profound gulf between themselves and the economically undeveloped nations, isolating themselves from the working masses of those nations. Everybody knows that being against assistance when the people desire it cannot be popular.

What then is the reason some Chinese communists adopt such an attitude? Clearly it lies in their sectarian and dogmatic view of the very concept of the socialist revolution in our time. Probably the following words of Lenin's could be applied to that concept:

"To imagine that the social revolution is *conceivable* without revolts by small nations in the colonies and in Europe, without the revolutionary outbursts of a section of the petty bourgeoisie *with all its prejudices*, without the movement of non-class-conscious proletarian and semi-proletarian masses against oppression of the landlords, the church, the monarchy, the foreign nations, etc.—to imagine that means *repudiating social revolution*. Only those who imagine that in one place an army will line up and say, 'we are for socialism', and in another place an army will say, 'we are for imperialism', and that this will be the social revolution, only those who hold such a ridiculous pedantic opinion, could vilify the Irish Rebellion by calling it a 'putsch'.

Whoever expects a 'pure' social revolution will *never* live to see it. Such a person pays lip service to revolution without understanding what revolution is."[1]

Thus, as always, so it is in the case of the Chinese attitude towards economic aid to underdeveloped countries; in practice ultra-radicalism in words offers impotence, opportunist kotowing to elemental forces, isolation from the masses and actual support of the forces of reaction.

In a similar light also appear the Chinese tactics regarding the question of disarmament.

Here is what Liu Chang Sheng said on the matter in June 1960, at a sitting of the General Council of the World Federation of Trade Unions:

"We support the proposal for disarmament which the Soviet Union has made. It is however out of the question that imperialism would accept a proposal for general and complete disarmament. The purpose of submitting such a proposal is to prompt the peoples of the whole world to unite and with their combined strength to oppose the imperialist plans for an armaments race and preparations

---

[1] Lenin: *Selected Works*, Cooperative Publishers. Moscow, 1935, English edition Vol. V, p. 303.

for war and to unmask the aggressive and bellicose nature of imperialism before the peoples of the world, so that as many as possible may isolate the imperialist bloc, with the United States of America at its head, so that it would not lightly dare provoke a war. But there are peoples who believe that such a proposal can be realized while imperialism still exists and that the danger of war can be removed by relying on such a proposal. This is an unreal illusion...

Only when the socialist revolution wins in the whole world can there be a world free from war, a world without armaments...

The Soviet Union and the other socialist countries should continue the development of their leadership in the field of atomic energy and at the same time the peoples in the whole world should lead a more decisive struggle against imperialism and against nuclear weapons. Solely in those circumstances could such an agreement be concluded.

But even when an agreement is concluded, it is still always possible that imperialism will treat it as a scrap of paper. And even if in their own interests the imperialists did not dare to begin an atomic war on a large scale, they may still begin a war with so-called conventional weapons."[1]

The plain question is indeed unavoidable: whether such "teachings" of the Chinese theoreticians about disarmament can be made to fit in with the principles on which the *Peace Manifesto* of November 23rd, 1957, signed among others also by the Chinese Communist Party, is based. For here is what we read there about this:

[1] According to the *Hsinhua Agency*, June 8, 1960.

"We representatives of communist and workers' parties, completely aware of our responsibility for the fate of the peoples, declare that war is not inevitable, war can be prevented, peace can be safeguarded and consolidated. . .

Nobody can deny that the proposals submitted to the United Nations for consideration regarding the curtailment of the armaments race and the removal of the danger of an atomic war, the peaceful coexistence of states, the development of economic cooperation between them, which constitute a decisive factor in the creation of the indispensable confidence in the relations between states, correspond to the vital interests of all peoples. To a great extent the fate of the world, the fate of future generations, is dependent on the settlement of these matters. These proposals come up against the active opposition of all those who have an interest in the maintenance of international tension . . .

The socialist countries will not impose their social or political system on any people by force. They are firmly convinced of the inevitable victory of socialism, but they are also aware that socialism cannot be implanted from outside, that it must above all be the result of the internal struggle of the working-class and all progressive forces in every country. Because of this the socialist countries are far from meddling in the internal relationships of other countries, though they also will not allow others to meddle in their internal affairs . . .

We address this appeal to all of you: demand the curtailment of the armaments race, which daily increases the danger of war, and falls heaviest on you, the workers."

In the meantime it is obvious that no changes have taken place in the world which would call for that radical change in the attitude to disarmament and peace which we observe today in the leaders of China, and which is in such sharp and obvious contradiction to the spirit and letter of the *Manifesto*. Consequently, we have to look for the causes of that change in their attitude in the Chinese themselves.

Judging by the Chinese view of things, nothing in international relations can be changed till the very last capitalist has vanished from the face of the earth. It is with this argument as starting-point that the Chinese theoreticians have so "interpreted" all the basic theses of the *Manifesto* that they have robbed them of any mobilizing force.

The point is that what is most important in any political tactics is that any aim one strives for should be a practical one. Otherwise the tactics themselves are doomed in advance to failure, and those who apply them to crushing defeat.

This means that the peoples can be mobilized around the problem of disarmament only if this constitutes a practical aim. Anybody who advocates a theory according to which the struggle for disarmament is only a tactical manoeuvre "to unmask somebody" not only immobilizes the strength of the "manoeuvre" itself, that is, makes it barren and ridiculous, but, viewing the matter objectively, also directly aids the most bellicose circles in the capitalist countries. This is precisely the result of the Chinese interpretation of the tactics regarding disarmament.

The Chinese theoreticians greatly underestimate the common sense of the Yugoslav communists when they ascribe to them the illusion that the problem of disarmament can be resolved by "persuasion". But still more do they underestimate the common sense of the Chinese communists when they ascribe to them the view that it will be possible, by the Chinese tactics regarding disarmament, to "unmask" anybody or anything in the world, except those tactics themselves.

This means that the result of these ultra-radical tactics too is impotence, passivity, and actual support of the forces of war.

Further, as for the assertion that even disarmed imperialism might begin a world war, that is to say, a war with the last remnants of conventional weapons, that indeed is a piece for a humorous magazine. It is not clear whether the Chinese authors of these theories really do feel this mystic fear of the "paper tiger", or are merely doing all they can to undermine the struggle for peace and disarmament by making it a subject for laughter. In any case, in what they do they are as alike as one pea to another to those American journalists who also, opposing the notion that disarmament is practical politics, wrote that even if completely disarmed the Chinese would be able to subjugate the whole world with only sticks and stones as weapons.

Connected with this too is the distinction which the Chinese writers make between the struggle for peace and the struggle for socialism, separating these "two struggles" and even setting one against the other.

Here are some excerpts from the Chinese press:

"The struggle for peace and the struggle for socialism are two distinct things. It is a mistake not draw a precise distinction between these two kinds of struggle. The social composition of those who take part in the movement for peace is unquestionably extremely complex. It even includes bourgeois pacifists... In this movement we shall join numerous complex social groupings and conclude necessary agreements for the achievement of peace. But at the same time we must stick to the principles of a party of the working-class and not lower our political or ideological standards in any way or reduce ourselves to the level of bourgeois pacifists in our struggle for peace. Here the question of alliance and criticism arises...

'Peace' on the lips of the modern revisionists is intended to cloak the war preparations of the imperialists and again to sing the old song of that 'ultra-imperialism' of the old revisionists, which Lenin long since rejected, to disrupt our communist policy regarding the peaceful coexistence of countries with two different systems and to reduce it to the elimination of people's revolutions in the various countries...

For this reason the 'peace' of which they speak is in practice reduced to a 'peace' which would be acceptable to the imperialists in certain historical circumstances. It is intended to lower the revolutionary standards of the peoples of the various countries and blunt the edge of their revolutionary will..."[1]

To what extent the whole historical sense of the struggle for peace and peaceful coexistence is twisted out of all shape in these phrases is plain enough from our preceding exposition. I do not consider it necessary to repeat those arguments here. But there are two aspects of the Chinese "tactics" in matters concerning the struggle for peace which do call for special emphasis.

[1] *The Red Flag*, according to the *Hsinhua Agency*, Peking, April 19, 1960.

What Is Revolutionary and What Is Not

For us, first and foremost, the struggle for peace and peaceful coexistence is merely one component of the struggle for socialism. It is not "another struggle", but the same struggle. It does not damp down, but on the contrary facilitates the struggle for socialism, progress and national independence in every country—by means which are appropriate to the conditions of that country. Moreover, it facilitates this struggle precisely by reducing to the minimum the possibilities of interference from outside.

But to the Chinese theoreticians the struggle for peace is some "other" sort of struggle. What sort? For peace in general? Obviously not, for that would very definitely be a barren pacifism. However, there is no need to tire ourselves seeking the content of this "other" struggle, because in fact there is none at all. In essence the Chinese theoreticians just do not consider the struggle for peace or coexistence to be a practical one at all, because they see the course of world revolution to be through inevitable war. For these reasons they reduce slogans about peace primarily to mere political catchwords "to unmask the bourgeoisie", in fact, just the same attitude as that regarding disarmament.

Further, the question again arises: what is likely to be the effect of the Chinese tactics in the struggle for peace if in advance that struggle is declared to be ineffective? And however can the working masses put their heart into the struggle for peace when in advance they are expected to count on the indispensability of having to take their places lined up on one side or the other of a "demarcation line" that is, of the war front between two worlds?

And, finally, what sort of alliance of the communists with other political groups in the struggle for peace is it going to be when those groups are informed that there is a difference of aims between their struggle for peace and that of the communists, and that this difference primarily consists in their believing in the feasibility of preserving peace while the communists do not believe in it, but merely wish to exploit that struggle for certain political ends of their own. In fact such an attitude leads to the direct undermining of the drive to consolidate peace.

These two questions alone are enough to illustrate how senseless and barren are the tactics which the Chinese "strategists" recommend. Exactly as Lenin said: one army on one side, another on the other, and so on.

No more than they, of course, do we cherish any illusions whatsoever about the peaceable nature of certain bellicose imperialist circles in the world. For this reason our conviction that the drive for peace as practical politics does not derive from any "confidence in imperialism", such as the Chinese critics charge us with. but from faith in the present-day ability of the socialist, progressive, democratic and all other peace-loving forces in the world to fight for and win a situation in which nobody would be able to infringe the peace without condemning themselves in advance to defeat. Now this is very different indeed from what the Chinese critics say about the essence of our struggle for peace.

This battle too, of course, cannot be finally won overnight. The danger of aggression will remain a real danger for a long time yet. But to the extent to which peace stimulates the internal struggle for socialism and social progress in each country, the results of that struggle will reinforce peace. For this reason we see in the struggle for peace precisely one of the instruments of the struggle for socialism.

This means that we come again to the same conclusion: the only fruit of the Chinese tactics in the struggle for peace is a lack of faith in peace, a passive expectation of war, a helpless contemplation of the grouping of the nations and of men into two fronts for a future "inevitable war". But this gives the bourgeoisie of the capitalist countries a chance to establish itself as the champion of the defence of national independence and on that platform further to gain the support of a great part or even the greater part of the working-class. Again ultra-radical language results in isolation and impotent contemplation of the course of events.

Finally, I will quote one more example of these Chinese tactics.

Speaking of the prospects of the struggle for socialism and for peace, the Chinese theoreticians of course justifiably point to the decisive role of the working-class of the capitalist countries. But of what working-class exactly are they thinking? They have in mind a working-class which they have fabricated in their dogmatic textbooks, one which everywhere is all impatience to welcome a world war, as its form of revolution. But today there is no such working-class as this. Further, the working-class which does exist is—as everybody knows—not a coherent unity even within its own national frontiers, let alone on a world scale. But what is above all important is *that it is for peace, against a world war, and cannot grasp that it is supposed to seize power by means of a world war and foreign armies.*

If therefore the role of the working-class in current social processes in the world and in the struggle for peace is to come fully to expression, it is essential for the leading socialist forces to apply political means and methods which are appropriate to the conditions of the moment and the structure of the working-class.

It is precisely this that the Chinese theoreticians are unable or do not wish to grasp. To them the working-class is—whoever unconditionally adopts the Chinese standpoint. Anybody who does not do this belongs to the reformist camp, the revisionist camp, the camp of betrayal of socialism, and this means the camp of imperialism.

However, the working-class of a country can be under the influence of reformism and yet be—indeed, it is—in favour of peace. And it can reject the Chinese recipes for the socialist revolution and yet nevertheless be an active factor in the struggle for socialism. For this reason it is senseless to the extreme simply to go on repeating historical truths about the "bourgeoisification of the proletariat" in certain countries, about a working-class aristocracy, about the opportunism of the whole working-class of certain nations, and expect a series of automatic changes in the views of this working-class. Long ago Marx and Lenin both made the observation that even the working-class is no absolute or monolithic category, but also is a process dependent on the development and structure of the forces of production as a whole, and since then not only has nothing been changed in those historical truths, but in their further development these have come still more to expression and been confirmed. Now, this fact in itself tells us that we are not here concerned with a problem which can be decided by ideological debate, that is, which can be transformed overnight, but a phenomenon which is ineluctably produced by the objective laws of social development. If revolutionary socialism wishes to remain on the solid ground of science and revolutionary realism, it must not merely take note of these facts, but also take account of them in its actual policy.

In other words, if the Chinese theoreticians do not think that the working-class of a certain country should be "improved" by force, it is certainly senseless and illusory of them to develop a policy based on barren expectations that the working-class of a country which, for instance, is hampered by opportunism and reformism will automatically mend its ways and free itself from opportunism, even · though the internal structure of the given society and working-class "produce" that opportunism, by the force of a natural law. This would mean condemning oneself to passivity and to complete political isolation. But that is just what is happening to present-day Chinese policy in a number of countries. It is incapable of winning the support of the working-class.

It is patently much more sensible to start from the actual state of things and seek points of contact with the working-class such as it is today, and this regarding those questions on which the aspirations and interests of the working-class of the whole world coincide, namely, in the defence of peace and the free development of socialism and social progress in every country by those means which the working-class of every country happens to choose. Such relationships do not exclude but, on the contrary, necessarily presuppose mutual criticism and a mutual ideological and political struggle, but at the same time they call for taking the totality of developments into consideration and certainly exclude forcing any views, no matter whose, on others by force, pressure or intimidation from outside.

Precisely in this sense should the struggle of the socialist forces for the greatest possible unity of the working-class or of the working-class movements of various ideological trends be built up over those points on which such unity is feasible.

This however is a problem which merits special, more detailed study. In the framework of this chapter I have mentioned it solely as an instance which shows how indispensable it is today for Marxists to free themselves from mechanically quoting the written word and instead, in the spirit of the basic scientific discoveries of Marxism, to grasp current events on the basis of an objective analysis of the facts, and in conformity with this to determine what weapons, instruments and methods of struggle for socialism are appropriate. It is quite clear that the material conditions for the further extension of socialism are today far more developed and favourable than the results achieved show. This is most likely a consequence mainly of the tremendous lag in socialist thought today, which has become fettered in a conservative dogmatism blind to the great changes which have taken place in the world. And precisely for this reason is it possible—as a reaction to this lagging behind of Marxist thought—for all sorts of wretched forms of abstract or muddle-headed Philistine pseudo-democratism, pseudo-humanism and pseudo-moralism to be represented as progressive currents.

All in all, both the tactics which the Chinese theoreticians advocate in the sphere of the struggle for the unity of the working-class on a world scale and those which they apply in the sphere of rallying the working-class in the internal struggle for socialism suffer from the same weaknesses as those other counsels of theirs about tactics which we have discussed. Such tactics frighten off large sections of the working-class, and condemn revolutionary socialism to isolation and a passive waiting for elemental changes, thereby in fact helping the bourgeoisie to find a common platform with greater or lesser portions of the working-class over foreign policy.

Ultra-radicalism in words and sectarian phraseology are no proof of a revolutionary quality, and still less are they the way to any real revolutionary results. In any case the working-class—least of all one which has behind it a long history of the class struggle—takes nobody's empty words at their face value. That is its great merit. Its confidence can be won only by that movement which in the long-lasting day-to-day struggle is capable of showing results in deeds.

CHAPTER 11

A Fateful Historical Dilemma

It is obvious that within the socialist world of our time a quite specific dilemma is crystallizing out regarding the further development of socialism as a world system. Namely, in resolving the contradictions between the two systems, one can either base oneself on the internal factors of socialism and of social progress in each country and on the international action of the socialist forces, within a system of coexistence, which is the only truly revolutionary and democratic concept of the struggle for socialism, or one can base oneself on the inevitability of war, a concept which bears within itself certain dangers of profound distortions and deviations in the development of socialism.

It would of course be out of place to discuss the personal intentions or aspirations of those responsible for Chinese foreign policy, for the dilemma cannot be reduced to the question of whether anybody "desires" or "does not desire" war. The decisive issue is the final effect in practice of any given policy. If we look at things in that light, a quite definite conclusion regarding the character of the Chinese concepts of war and peace is unavoidable. Namely, whether the Chinese theoreticians want this or not, the inner logic of the Chinese attitude inevitably leads to basing oneself on the second way of "resolving" the world contradictions, namely, on resolution by war.

Today there are two huge armed camps facing one another, each with a tremendous potential of material destruction and of annihilation of the vital forces of mankind. A course based on the inevitability of a war between these two camps means a course set for the further building up of that destructive power to an extent at which the mere existence of the antagonistically aimed war potentials would of itself become a possible cause of war. In such circumstances the most simple-minded of men must be aware that a line of policy based on the inevitability of war in fact means a line based on war, including here an offensive war. There can be no question but that such a line arms the most reactionary protagonists of war and on the other hand weakens the forces of peace and coexistence. In other words, the mere basing of one's policy on the inevitability of war in the circumstances of today in effect serves to strengthen the forces of imperialism and the forces of war, becomes indeed a form of instigation to war. It goes without saying that such a direction of policy cannot but subordinate to itself the whole internal and foreign policy of the country which adopts such a course.

From this further derives the characteristic Chinese criticism of present-day drives for peace and disarmament. To be genuinely in favour of peace is in the view of these critics to be a pacifist, to deal with illusions, if not indeed to "render assistance to imperialism". To have genuine faith in the possibility of disarmament and not see in proposals for disarmament merely a propaganda manoeuvre means disseminating illusions. The Chinese theoreticians are not aware that thereby they are declaring the whole struggle

167

for socialism to be an illusion, for the struggle for peace is an inseparable part of the struggle for socialism.

Of course we are not in favour of peace in the abstract and against war in the abstract, but for a quite concrete peace and against a quite concrete war. In 1941 we Yugoslav communists were not in favour of peace but of war, whereas the Yugoslav bourgeoisie at the time was for peace. But today the problem is quite different. I repeat: *the fateful dilemma of world socialism today lies first in the question whether the principal international political contradiction of the world of our time, that between the world of socialism and the world of capitalism, must inevitably be resolved by a new world war, or whether it will gradually find its solution in a process of internal social developments in the various countries,* and secondly, in the question whether the forces of socialism today are sufficiently strong to be able by peace and a stable system of coexistence to insist on another path of resolution of that contradiction, that is, the path of internal social progress which, viewed politically and historically, is the only way which corresponds to the spirit and the direct interests of socialism and modern human civilization.

Here is the essence of the struggle for peace and for this reason it cannot be treated otherwise than as a part of the struggle for socialism, just as real as any other part of that struggle. Apart from this, socialism has in principle always been for peace and only for peace. In itself socialism is a synonym of lasting peace, for in itself it bears that strength which tomorrow will eliminate all the sources of war. Socialism accepts solely those defensive revolutionary and people's liberation wars which are imposed by the forces of reaction and imperialism, or result from the indispensable struggle against these. This means that socialism is not in favour of peace merely tomorrow, but peace now, today, in so far as this is objectively possible that is, in so far as the matured forces of socialism already make peace possible today. It would be senseless and quite anti-socialist to assert that with the growth of the forces of socialism the inevitability of war is increased, for this would mean asserting that socialism itself is a source of war.

Socialism, if one means genuine socialist social relationships and not elements of the old in the new, not only cannot be a source of war, but its consolidation in the world should be a factor making for a lessening of the danger of war, a factor making for elimination of the inevitability of war. To assert the opposite would be to admit that the policy of a socialist country is governed by anti-socialist, hegemonistic views.

This does not mean that we appeal to pacifism at the cost of social progress, to the detriment of socialist solidarity and the support which a socialist and democratic country should offer the forces of progress, democracy and revolution. As we saw above, coexistence is no invitation to capitulation before aggression nor is it an obstacle to the revolutionary struggle. On the contrary, it facilitates the struggle of the progressive social forces.

Of course, 1 do not mean by this to assert that it is possible to separate the internal social processes, revolutionary or other, from international relations, particularly not from the basic contradictions of the world of today, the opposition between the two systems, by a Chinese wall. That would be quite unrealistic. The relationship of forces on a world scale is primarily decided by the internal development in each country. For this reason every revolutionary and liberational struggle, every drive for economic and political independence, acquires a more or less international significance and engages international forces which, of course, for their part again influence the internal social processes. In this sense we are unquestionably living in a period of a continuous process of world revolution, a process which unfolds in the most varied forms and which by every new move forward in this or that way affects the social forces of all peoples. Peoples no longer develop isolated one from another, each to itself, but in a definite world environment with which they are connected by countless threads of mutual influence and mutual dependence.

However, to see only this aspect of the movement and determine one's political action solely by these factors of world development would be to deceive oneself and expose oneself to the danger of serious defeats.

The social development of mankind today, taken as a whole, is determined by two basic processes. On the one hand there unfolds a process of centralization of the process of linking together, of fusing, of uniting and of ever greater mutual dependence on a world scale, which is a consequence of the present-day state and development of the forces of production and the need for an ever broader and more intensive and more planned international division of labour; while on the other hand there unfolds a process of building up of the autonomy of the individual—of peoples as of persons—of all manner of social activities, and by this also of the demand for their decentralization, which is the expression of the degree of socialization of the process of labour, as also of the need for further advancement of the social-economic relationships between men. Both these processes are two inseparable sides of the same social movement. The socialist forces must take account of them, both in internal and in foreign policy.

To see only the first aspect in internal politics is to sink into a bureaucratic-*étatiste* conservatism and to hamper the activity of men in the development of the productive forces, while to see only the other side is to go back to a bourgeois pseudo-liberalism, surrendering to the elemental and disarming the conscious forces of social advance.

In foreign policy the first case leads to an overestimation of the influence of the contradictions between the two world systems on the internal revolutionary and other social processes, and may even lead to the conclusion that at the present time the hegemony of this or that socialist state or group of socialist states or a world war is the most practical weapon for further advancement of the world revolution, and that the internal revolutionary and other progressive forces are incapable of winning victory independently. The other case equally in foreign policy leads to the abandonment of things to elemental forces, and this means their abandonment to reactionary factors and changing the relationship of the social forces in the world to the advantage of those factors.

In both one and the other case the persons responsible for such one-sided courses of policy expose themselves to the danger of serious defeats, while they are also likely to inflict serious distortions on socialist development.

But when we examine both these processes in their mutual interconnectedness it is clear that it is still the internal social forces of the various countries or of various peoples that remain the basic prime mover of social progress and of the further socialist transformation of the world. The international significance of all these internal social processes does not arise from their nature itself but from their influence on the relationship of the social forces on a world scale. This indeed only goes to confirm our thesis that precisely because the internal revolutionary, anti-imperialist and other progressive processes of today necessarily acquire an international significance, they will unfold so much more quickly and so much more ineluctably, more easily and less painfully in each separate country, the more stable world peace is, and *vice versa*, that the greater the international tension and instability, the greater will be the pressure which stifles the internal social and revolutionary processes. This means that in the circumstances of today every step in the direction of the stabilization of peace at the same time means a step farther in the strengthening of the forces of socialism, progress and democratic cooperation between the nations.

In other words, the necessary internationalist function of the socialist states in assisting the progressive processes in the world consists not in the imposition of their hegemony or their systems on others, but first and foremost in using their own strength to prevent war or interference in the internal affairs of other countries, to ensure democratic relationships between nations, to ensure the stabilization of peace and the peaceful coexistence of nations, independently of their systems. The struggle for these aims in international relations is at the present day an organic part of the struggle of the progressive forces inside every country. Whatever the international significance of the internal progressive social processes of today, they always unfold within the framework of a definite world relationship of forces. If the balance of that relationship should tip in favour of the peace-loving forces, the further struggle for socialism in an ever greater part of the world in no way imposes the conclusion that a war between the states of the two world systems is inevitable.

As far as support of the progressive and anti-imperialist movements goes, one needs merely once again draw attention to the words of Lenin's quoted above about the limits of the aid which a socialist country can give to such movements in other countries. It is unquestionable that even today this attitude of Lenin's has lost nothing of its importance, but has rather gained in importance. This attitude in no way shows Lenin to have been more indifferent to the revolutionary movements in other countries than the Chinese communists are today. It merely confirms that Lenin based the prospects of world socialism on the internal revolutionary and generally progressive forces of the individual countries, and not on wars or on the imposition of socialism from outside.

It would of course unquestionably be an illusion to believe that in the circumstances of today it will be possible to attain rapid results as regards the stabilization of peace or coexistence.

However, here it is not at all speed or time that is in question, but whether the line of policy based on peace, on coexistence, on disarmament, and so forth, in present-day circumstances that is, in the period before the disappearance

173

of the very last capitalist from the globe, is a practical one or not. Further, it is also a matter of whether it is practical politics to argue that the preservation of peace means leading imperialism itself up a blind alley, thereby speeding up internal progressive social movements in the direction of the final liquidation of the remnants of that system. If the first is possible, then so is the second a possibility.

In other words, the question is not whether a long or a short time is necessary for such a policy or whether there is great possibility or a slight one of its realization, but merely whether such a possibility exists or does not exist. If it does, it is the sacred duty of all the socialist forces to fight for its realization, not forgetting, of course, the opposite possibility, that is, that the forces of war may still prove to be more powerful. However, this other possibility should not be allowed to weaken our efforts to realize the first possibility.

In contradistinction to such views, the Chinese theoreticians, as we have seen, advance the argument that the struggle for peace and the struggle for socialism are two different struggles. The Chinese theoreticians clearly consider, in addition to what we have already brought out, that the struggle for peace falls exclusively in the sphere of agitation, propaganda, explaining things to people, unmasking and so on and so forth, while the struggle for socialism falls in the sphere of the real, material transformation of things. Consequently, if we aim at changing things by the inevitability of war, the policy of peace cannot but come into conflict with the struggle for socialism.

The leadership of the Communist Party of China obviously subordinates all the other questions of socialist policy to this line based on the inevitability of war. In that line of policy, indeed, may be seen the fundamental source of those sectarian-ultra-radical and dogmatic attitudes, which we have already discussed, which that leadership assumes on matters of concrete tactics in the international policy of socialism.

It is no accident that such views should have appeared today. The Chinese communists thereby spontaneously and unwittingly react to those very changes in the quantitative relationship of the social forces which they claim do not introduce anything new into the world of today.

However, precisely those great changes, being the result of the growth in the strength of socialism, now again in a new form make the question of the paths and the means for the further development of socialism, an immediate one. Clearly both forms and paths have multiplied in number and the means too have become more numerous. But even though they may be considered to be Marxists, all men do not react in the same way to such changes. Further, they do not react in the same way because Marxism and Socialism are as an ideology only one factor of those reactions, the other factor being the external conditions in which the conscience of the leading social factors is formed. Consequently, for special social trends to be explained it is far from sufficient to be satisfied with offering them up to Marxism, one should also have in mind the other circumstances, both objective and subjective, which have influenced the formation of the particular policy.

In his day Trotsky strove to assist the war of the Soviet Union with the capitalist countries, which he thought inevitable, by world revolution. That was a reflection of the weakness of socialism and of lack of faith in the strength of the socialist revolution. Now the Chinese communists hope that war will assist the world revolution, since they consider that there is an inevitable connection between the one and the other. This is a reflection of the strength of socialism and at the same time of lack of faith in the revolutionary forces of other countries. But the practical result in the two cases is the same: it boils down to a short-sighted attempt to solve the internal difficulties of the revolution at the cost of subordinating the world interests of socialism to the supposed momentary interests of a particular socialist country.

Of course, the mutual assistance of the socialist forces in the spirit of socialist internationalism and solidarity is one of the basic factors of socialist developments in the world. But when someone wishes to impose certain specific interests, even if these are justified—but the more so if they are not—on the international socialist movement by force, socialist internationalism ceases and a struggle for domination begins, that is, as Lenin put it, an attempt at "riding on somebody else's shoulders" for the satisfaction of one's own "selfish interests".

The present period favours the appearance of such trends. Moreover, the problem becomes acute by the mere fact that the relationship of the social forces on a world scale is gradually changing to the advantage of socialism. This fact is bound to set into action powerful progressive movements in the socialist ranks in the sense of opening up new prospects for socialism. But it will also set into action negative phenomena, and particularly two of them. First, there will be men who will consider that the present-day strength of socialism should be used in order "finally" to settle the fate of the contradiction between socialism and capitalism in a war which is in any case "inevitable". And there will be men who apart from this, deliberately or unwittingly, will be inclined to see the strength of socialism used not in harmony with the interests of world socialism, but to satisfy some egoistic or narrowly understood special or nationalistic interest of this or that country. It goes without saying that if such trends forced their way into socialist international and internal policies they would cause grave distortions in socialist development and for a certain period would markedly weaken the forces of socialism. This is indeed precisely where lies the world historical significance of the dilemma under discussion.

CHAPTER 12

War and Socialism

For all these reasons, in this fateful historical dilemma between a policy based on coexistence and a policy based on the inevitability of world war the problem whether to take one decision or the other is not merely a problem of responsibility for the sacrifices and devastation which war would bring the nations and civilization in our day, nor is it merely the problem of the immediate political repercussions on the attitude of humanity in general to socialism, least of all is it merely a problem of ethics and politics, but it is before all else the problem of the paths of further development of socialism as a world-wide system.

This is why we need to make a special study of this problem.

In the first place, we need to be quite clear about an illusion which has taken complete possession of the minds of Chinese theoreticians. For they maintain that the "united socialist world" which would arise tomorrow, as the result of a postulated third world war, would mean "the end to all war", "the end of armament", "the end of conflict", in short, that there would emerge a world of wonderful harmony which would tend to the creation of "a truly glorious future" for the peoples of the world. There is no gainsaying it—were the result to be such, it might be justifiable to take upon oneself the responsibility for the sacrifices which a new world war would involve.

178

However, we have here a grave illusion, so grave that one really does wonder how men who consider themselves Marxists could ever have succumbed to it. For above all a Marxist should know that in the last resort it is the state of the forces of production that constitutes the factor which determines the nature and form of the relationships between men.

According to all we know today in the field of war technology, a third world war would not be at all the same as the First and Second World Wars were. In many aspects modern military techniques change the nature of warfare and the social-economic consequences of war qualitatively. One does not need to be an extreme pessimist, and imagine a third world war to be the end of the world, to be none the less conscious of the fact that today a world war could not but be a war of mass annihilation. Now who can say today what political forces would result or how these would act if the whole world economy were catastrophically destroyed? For the Chinese theoreticians it is sufficient to make the assertion that the result would be socialism.

But even were we to suppose this to be indisputable— whereas in fact it would cease to be indisputable the moment the socialist countries tried to impose their system on the others—we must not forget that socialism by itself, as a word, is not a magician's wand which abolishes every evil, which overnight creates an abundancy of commodities, which makes men good, which puts an end to contradictions and antagonisms and conflicts among men, from the first day of the revolution, even after a destructive war. A war of that sort would bring annihilation principally to the most developed parts of the world, which—at least in certain fields—might well result in a catastrophic lowering of the level of world productive forces for a certain period thereby setting up important new contradictions between one country and another, as well as contradictions within each country. In a world socialist system based on productive forces which were undeveloped and at the same time catastrophically destroyed, with vestiges of hegemony, nationalism, inequalities between nations and so forth still lingering on, the development of socialism would be a complex process, in which for a certain time those vestiges would not merely inevitably continue but would in many a case gain in strength. And that would be a process which for a considerable time would ineluctably also maintain and further develop those antagonizing contradictions, lending the remnants of the old social system fresh incentives and nourishment.

In other words, history would take her revenge on anybody who by the enforced export of socialism tried to ignore the objective laws of social development by instilling this new "united" world socialist system, established and maintained by war and hegemony, with those contradictions for the elimination of which the hour would be premature, since the development of the productive forces of the world would not have made this feasible. For this reason any development of socialism under such conditions could not fail to be accompanied by great deformations.

The Chinese illusions about a post-war "harmony" thus have the same source as all the other theories which have already been discussed. For by equating war and revolution, they forget that international war has its own laws, and revolution others.

But still more important is another aspect of this question.

It is customary to say that foreign policy is a reflection of home policy. The contrary, however, is also true. Foreign policy has definite consequences in both internal social developments and in political developments. This holds good both for capitalist and socialist countries, although these processes unfold in different ways in these two fields. But above all both one and the other policy have a great influence on the development of socialism as a world system, which in its very nature is the product of the interlocking of very complex processes, forms, and paths. *This very complexity is at the same time socialism's wealth, that is, that internal force which makes it possible for those processes to interlock and mutually criticize each other, and so to ensure the greatest vigour and rapidity of development. Anything that damps down that vigour, that tends to uniformity and monopolism, acts as a brake on these developments.*

"Proletarian revolutions", wrote Marx in *The 18th Brumaire of Louis Bonaparte*, . . . "on the other hand constantly... criticize themselves, interrupt themselves continually in their own course, come back to the apparently accomplished in order to begin it afresh, deride with unmerciful thoroughness the inadequacies, weaknesses and paltrinesses of their first attempts . . ."[1]

At the present time the problem of a free choice of paths and forms of socialist development is certainly gaining in importance. Considered as a social-economic category in the course of history, there is of course in principle only

[1] Marx-Engels: *Selected Works*, International Publishers, New York, Vol. II, p. 319.

one socialism. But feudalism, capitalism and other social systems are also quite precise categories, but none the less the paths and forms by which they arose and developed were most multifarious. The same applies to socialism all the more, since here we have a process of inception and development of a classless society, consequently the process is so much more complex.

What is more, *the problems of the contradictions between the world of socialism and the world of capitalism will gradually acquire a secondary significance, while the problems of the further development of socialist social relations will increasingly become the real history of our age.* True, it would be a mistake today to underestimate the importance of these contradictions, since the forces of capitalism are still powerful, but it would be a still greater mistake to think that by saying that this or that country is a socialist country we have said everything. The same battle is fought out on the socialist ground too, even though in different forms, and this at the same time is all interlocked with the internal contradictions of socialist development itself, and it is precisely this that in the transitional stage makes it possible for hegemonistic trends, national egoisms, bureaucratic monopolism and so forth, to appear.

The contradictions between the world of socialism and the world of capitalism, it goes without saying, are with all the inevitability of a natural process—parallel with the economic consolidation of socialism—bound to acquire the character of a gradual overcoming of the remnants of the old world. That development will be realized through manifold internal processes, political and social, both in the capitalist and in the socialist countries, by processes which will be further speeded up by the influence exerted by the international role of socialism, as this finds expression in various forms of cooperation and division of labour among the nations, as also in all forms of influence by example and experience.

The very variety of both objective and human factors, which go to make the concrete forms or paths of socialism so multifarious; the varied nature of the starting-points of socialist development in the various countries, which results in a great variety of modes and intensities of the interweaving of elements of the new and the old; and finally, the political and social-economic indispensability of every country— independently of the level of its material starting-point— uninterruptedly further developing socialist relationships if it wishes to maintain the unity of the working-class and the people—all this means that *the maximum of liberty in the selection of paths and forms of socialist development—on the basis of scientific socialist theory and the totality of the practical experience of socialism—is the first and the most significant condition of the healthy and rapid development of socialism as a world system,* and at the same time the first and most important condition for the suppression of that conservatism which accompanies any monopoly, in the political system of a socialist country just as much as in any other social system.

It is precisely for this reason that the dilemma between a course based on coexistence and a course based on the inevitability of war becomes of such great importance for all the socialist forces in the world. A policy which in its final consequences bears in itself any element of Bonapartism is harmful not merely from the standpoint of that reaction which it is likely to excite in the non-socialist countries, which we have already discussed, but above all from the standpoint of the further development of socialism. In itself this policy would be a reflection of definite deformations of socialist development in any country in which such trends appeared, and, further, if such a policy did appear, it would also begin to play its own independent role in the sense of a further deepening of those deformations in the world socialist system.

Here in fact above all arises the question—in the name of what concept of socialism—and experience has already shown how varied socialist practice can be—is this policy of conquering the world for socialism by means of war to be conducted? Secondly, there arises the question whether such a socialism—a socialism imposed by war, in forms which do not correspond to the actual social-economic structure of a country—can play any objectively progressive role at all, or whether it would not even stifle the development of the forces of production. For it is this last factor that is the determining measure of whether or not any social system, even a socialist one, is progressive.

If we view socialism not as a sort of perfect social ideal, but as the process of the gradual transformation of social relationships in harmony with development, with the social ownership of the means of production, then the contradiction which is characteristic of the world today is not one between an abstract socialism which is absolutely good and an abstract capitalism which is absolutely bad, but between a definite socialist system *in process of inception* and a definite capitalist system, *which is in decay.* Consequently, no objective Marxist analyst, appraising the actual state of international policy in our day and the tasks before it, would take account merely of the qualitative character of the contradiction, but would also take account of its quantitative aspects, that is, of those of its features which are relative, transitory and subject to change and which by their changing prepare for a decisive revolutionary "leap". But what forms that leap will assume is dependent on the internal social structure of a particular country, that is, precisely on the state of the "quantitative relationships" which hold in the moment of any revolutionary transformation.

Marx wrote that it is not the task of the proletarian revolution to realize some sort of "preconceived ideal", but solely to liberate those elements of the new society which are already conceived in the bosom of the old society. If we look at things not statically, but considered as this process of which Marx speaks, it is clear that within the "old" many elements of the "new" are already maturing. Here we are faced above all with a series of factual premises, material and social-economic, which tend increasingly to exacerbate the internal contradictions of capitalism and make socialism an ever more necessary way out of the general crisis of human society.

One such factor, for instance, is the ever more powerfully expressed social character of production. In Marx's day this feature found expression almost wholly within the individual capitalist factory. But even at that time Marx could point to the phenomenon of share companies and large capitalist concerns which had begun to plan more and more extensive complexes of production, as proof of the ever more powerful expression of the social character of labour in our age. In recent decades all these processes have gone much farther. Despite the fact that capitalist ownership still exists, the consequences of the social nature of labour ever more compellingly give rise to a whole system of social integration and social direction in the development of industry. This, it goes without saying, does not of itself change the nature of capitalist social-economic relationships. And, what is still more important, such integration is effected precisely in the interests of the maintenance of those relationships. But none the less this is a convincing proof to what extent the elemental forces of capitalist relationships are already subordinated to the pressure of a factor *which is external to them*, and with what speed, for this reason, the process of their internal decay is proceeding.

Another such factor is the decay of colonial empires and the establishment of the principle of national independence. This factor markedly narrows down the sphere of the economic and political hegemony of imperialism, and also the struggle for the imperialist partition of the world. At the same time it exerts a concrete material and political pressure in the sense of bringing about new forms of international economic relationships and an international division of labour, which all constitutes a further consequence of the social nature of labour on an international scale. Of course, all this does not of itself abolish imperialism, still less capitalist relationships, but it does show to what extent the material basis of imperialism has shrunk and that it will continue to shrink.

A third such factor may be found in the field of international economic and political relationships, in which the centre of gravity is increasingly passing to the socialist forces. It is precisely in this respect that the relationship of the social forces of the world has essentially changed since Lenin's time. Lenin saw the strength of socialism in its politically progressive character and influence, and its main weakness in its economic insignificance. For this reason he held that the Soviet Union would not exercise any influence by its economic strength, but that its political influence, its embodiment of the victorious revolution, would be of such a nature that it would largely tend to tie the hands of the forces of imperialism and war.

Today the situation is quite different. Socialism, as far as it acts in a consistently socialist way, will exert an influence both as a political and as an economic force. Socialism has become a powerful economic factor, and as such will assume an increasingly important role in the international division of labour, and thereby alone also in all international relationships. What is more, that economic factor will be—indeed, is already becoming—a most important political factor, for the simple reason that it is more capable of influencing the internal social-economic processes in the world of today than any general political propaganda. Those Marxists who do not see these facts merely prove that either in their dogmatic conservatism or in their short-sighted *ad hoc* way of understanding things they have become incapable of making any Marxist analysis of the real facts.

Now this, especially if it is taken together with the consequences of the decay of colonialism of which I have spoken above, means that *the very nature of international relationships—as arising from the given quantitative relationship of the social forces in the world—no longer tends to stimulate and strengthen the forces of imperialism, but on the contrary, narrows them down, limits them, hampers them, thereby making the internal crisis of capitalism all the more profound.*

Other similar factors could be listed. Everybody knows that the process of the decay of capitalism does not find expression merely in a direct conflict between the working-class and the heads of capitalist moponolies and the capitalist state, but can be seen also in the most varied forms of conflict about the set-up of the machinery of the state, about democratic institutions, about the role of state or social supervision of the planning of the direction of industrial development. The process is also apparent in the important standing now enjoyed by the working-class movement, also in its differentiation, which is the reflection of the various objective conditions in which the struggle for power of the working-class develops; it is apparent again in the struggle of the working-class in the mechanism of the state and of industry, in the standing acquired by anti-imperialistic and various other progressive movements, in the growth of the influence of so-called "public opinion" in the life of the community, which to a far greater extent than formerly is a reflection of the interests of the basic body of the people, and so forth. Of course, the determining factor is the working-class together with other progressive and anti-imperialist forces, which should liberate all those material processes, that is, which by means of the socialist and progressive forces should also win a political victory.

To summarize briefly, all these factors taken together increasingly hamper, narrow down and curtail the possibilities for the manifestation of what are precisely the most essential aims of imperialism, thereby bringing imperialism to a state of crisis, and so speed up its internal decay and strengthen the forces of socialism. To introduce a war policy into those processes would be to halt them and lend new strength to imperialism and all the reactionary social forces, which under such conditions would appear as the leading forces of defence of national independence.

On the other hand, the very development of social relationships in the socialist countries can no longer be defined exclusively in terms of the contradiction between socialism and capitalism understood in a narrow sense which I might qualify as pre-revolutionary. Contradictions are born, springing from the very soil of socialist development in the transitional period, which can no longer be connected with any manifest vestiges of the old order. Even in socialism there is no end to progress.

I have in mind above all such contradictions as the following:

1. the necessity for social ownership of the means of production to appear for a certain time in the form of state ownership, which gives birth to a tendency to preserve the state hired-labour relationship;

2. the necessity for a certain time for the socialist forces to rely on the force of the state, which gives birth to a trend towards the establishment of bureaucratism and also a tendency for *étatiste* deformations of socialist economic relationships;

3. the necessity for relationships between one socialist country and another to be founded on interstate relationships, which makes possible tendencies towards a desire to dominate others, to national egoism and like phenomena;

4. the necessity for socialism in the world in the initial phases to be developed on the basis of a very varied degree of economic development, which on the one hand gives rise to aspirations to maintain economic advantages, and on the other hand, to aspirations to settle economic differences by force or by pressure at the expense of others;

5. the necessity for the distribution of the products of labour for a long time to be made according to work done, to qualifications, or even according to the degree of immediate responsibility in the process of production and so forth, all of which tends to retain and will for a quite long time do so, not merely inequality in the material relationships between men, but also the need for more or less state interference in economic relations, and even, in some countries, definite features of state-capitalist relationships, and all this again tends to give birth to a bureaucratic tendency to maintain such relationships and economic differences, even under conditions which make feasible a gradual change in things;

6. the necessity by which the revolution gives birth to political monopoly and this in an elemental way strives to perpetuate itself, not only in the sphere of the defence of socialism against the restoration of capitalism, in which in many countries it will be necessary for quite a long time, but also in the sphere of economic and ordinary human relationships;

7. the necessity, in the work of resolution of social contradictions, of applying the objective scientific controls which Marxism has placed in the hands of the working-class, as against the prevailing empiricism which characterizes class systems (which of course does not mean that

science has played no part whatsoever at all in these), this necessity at the same time giving birth to a tendency towards the dogmatization of Marxism and the creation of an ideological monopoly, in the interests of the preservation of certain transitory and out-dated socialist forms and relationships.

And so on. Many other such examples could be listed.

Consequently, socialist development is effected through socialism's own internal objective contradictions, of some of which men are able more or less consciously to keep control, but not others, their own mentality being under the influence of those factual trends of development. It would be more than ridiculous to presuppose that after the revolution men all at once become so clever and so independent of material trends that their minds can grasp the whole complex of social and material developments, and direct them all with complete scientific precision. Still more ridiculous would it be to presuppose that by the mere fact of being the governments of a socialist country the government of this or that state is automatically endowed with an exceptional gift for appreciation of the absolute truth. Even in socialism the policy of any government should be judged by the factual results obtained in the advancement of socialist relationships, for it is only by such achievements that one can also find an indication to what extent any government has in fact proved capable of finding a creative basis in science.

Those Marxists who think that Engels' words about transition from the realm of necessity to the realm of liberty are realized on the morrow of the revolution have a completely mistaken, static conception of what Engels meant.

Whoever is concerned with the spirit, not with the factual phraseology of Marxism, is aware that here too Engels' formulation is to be taken merely as a formulation reflecting a process, and is no more than that. In other words, however much Marxism and the subsequent development of the science of socialism may have equipped conscious social forces to effect the conscious resolution of contradictions, they still do not endow them with the gift of any "absolute wisdom" which might enable them absolutely to understand and direct all social developments, that is, to be capable of rising absolutely above them, thereby acquiring criteria of supernatural wisdom. It is thus as clear as daylight that there will always "remain" contradictions in socialism, which will continue to appear as the elemental pressure of the objective facts on the social conscience.

Of course, contradictions of this sort do not inevitably acquire the form of a class struggle nor do they inevitably find their resolution by the clash of their contradictions, yet neither are they resolved by any sort of ideal plan or ideal government policy, but first and foremost by the clash of personal interests and by the struggle of opinions. Under such conditions conservatism, as a material and ideological force, is just as law governed a phenomenon as is the unrestrainable birth of tendencies to seek the way to a more rapid development of the material basis and towards more progressive forms of social relationships. In the present time these processes are very often complicated by the fact that to those contradictions the solution of which is possible and which should be solved in a democratic, evolutionary way, are complicated by political vestiges of the old social forces and their ideology which are directly linked to the world of capitalism. And the pressure of these influences acts as a brake on development, especially by creating the need for the more or less definite establishment of a socialist state, as a control of social relationships by force. In this process certain contradictions can even acquire the character of real conflict. Yet all the same this phenomenon should not conceal from us the fact that contradictions do exist and do act within the socialist relationships of the transitional period, even independently of any pressure, great or small, of vestiges of the old society.

It is quite clear that all these processes will unfold the less painfully and the more democratically and so much the more rapidly, the more freely every nation is in a position independently to choose the ways and forms of its own socialist development. The experience of the practice of the development of socialism as a whole and the objective scientific analysis of this will in this way also be the most powerful ideological stimulus for any individual socialist country on the path of advancement of socialist relationships.

The further expansion of world socialism will certainly not proceed and cannot proceed by any mechanical extension of the forms of those socialist relationships which have held or which hold today in the socialist countries, but rather by the birth of new forms, forms which are often also superior to those which existed before, provided the material basis has made such advancement possible. This on the other hand means that socialism will continue to force its way through in the capitalist countries by the most varied paths and in the most varied forms, which will at the same time not only enlarge the sphere of socialism but also have its influence in the sense of the further advancement of socialist forms within the existing socialist countries.

A war of the socialist countries with the purpose of forcibly implanting socialism on others would without question for a certain period establish a definite political hegemony and an ideological monopoly over the socialist countries and the development of world socialism. For this reason it is clear that such a war would be a reactionary factor precisely from the standpoint of socialist development.

Consequently, solely a defensive war of the socialist world against aggression and no other war whatsoever could—beside people's liberation and internal revolutionary wars—be defined as progressive, justified war.

It is precisely for this reason that the international policy of a socialist country should not allow any ambiguity whatsoever in regard to its attitude to the basic dilemma of mankind in our time, the dilemma of peace or war, which today concretely means the dilemma between adopting a course based on coexistence and a course based on the inevitability of war.

CHAPTER 13

On the Relations between Socialist Countries

The problem of the imposing of socialism by force from outside is at the same time a problem of the relations between socialist countries. For in principle, if socialism can be imposed on a non-socialist country, it is also possible to impose this or that form of internal development or this or that internal or external policy on a socialist country. The Chinese anti-Yugoslav campaign is a form of pressure in just this sense.

The question arises on what principles—under such conditions—the Chinese theoreticians imagine the relations between socialist countries should be founded. *For the democratic principles of cooperation and unity on a basis of equality of rights they obviously substitute another principle, in other words, that of the exercise of hegemony by certain nations.* But this does not merely mean opening the door to all manner of great-power tendencies in the relations between socialist countries, but also the exacerbation of conflicts between one nation and another. In the last resort such relations could only lead to a grim resurrection within the socialist world of certain methods of imperialist policy.

These arguments I would like to illustrate by two examples of practical consequences of the theories of the Chinese theoreticians whom we are discussing.

The first example concerns the internal social-economic development of China of today, first of all the system of the "people's communes" of China. The Chinese theoreticians—to judge by their own explanations—consider those communes one of the most advanced forms—if not the most advanced—in the development of world socialism, and recommend them to others.

Of the significance of those communes they write:

"The basic aim of the institution of the people's communes is to speed up the rate of socialist construction, while the aim of the realization of socialism is the active preparation of a transition to communism. It appears that the realization of communism in China is not a matter of the distant future. We should make energetic use of the form of the people's communes to examine the practical possibilities of a transition to communism."[1]

And in another place:

"Though in the people's communes for the present we mainly have collective ownership, which is rather of a socialist character, that membership already contains elements of common national ownership which will develop uninterruptedly and in from three to four or five to six years will completely transform collective ownership. The people's commune is for the present still of a socialist character, but will become the best organizational form for the construction of socialism and the gradual transition to communism. For this reason the establishment of the people's communes constitutes an event of great historical significance."[2]

Such assertions are indeed classic examples of subjectivist thought, for all they can express is the view that it

[1] *Resolution of the Central Committee of the Communist Party of China*, September 16, 1958.
[2] Leading article in the *Jen min ji bao* newspaper of September 1, 1958, entitled *All-people's holiday, all-people's victory*, according to the *New China* agency.

is possible to build up communism simply by the further elaboration of political forms, quite independently of the development of the forces of production.

But the fact is that these "people's communes" in China today are the political reflection of the efforts, politically conditioned, but temporary and transitory, of an insufficiently developed revolutionary country to create the economic foundations for the development of socialism. In other words, they are not yet socialism at all, but merely a material preparation for building socialism.

Of the essence of the communes such passages as the following, taken from Chinese writers, speak convincingly:

"In the people's communes the organization of labour is being militarized, the whole of their activity is realized in a combative spirit, life is collectivized, which corresponds to the demands of the present situation when a great leap ahead is being realized."[1]

"To have free meals and at the same time receive regular monthly income constitutes an event of world significance. Since the time when Marx put forward the noble ideal of communism, there have been those who have opposed it, with the argument that the pursuance of a policy the principle of which is 'from each according to his abilities, to each according to his needs' would create lazy people. Facts have shown that this is not the case. The introduction of a system of distribution which consists in giving people part of their wages in kind, while part is paid out in money and tokens, has freed people from worry about food and clothing. Now people's principal concern is how to work still better,

---

[1] An article in the *Jen min ji bao* newspaper of October 1, 1958, entitled *All-people's holiday, all-people's victory;* according to the *New China* agency.

to be worthy of the new society, and to demonstrate their gratitude to the Communist Party and President Mao Tse-tung. People have not become lazy. On the contrary, they have become still more diligent and work with greater enthusiasm and fire. It looks as if with the gradual introduction of a communist economic system both the communist conscience and the morale of the people act one on the other."[1]

The *Jen min ji bao* of September 10, 1958 further emphasized:

"Pay according to work done is a remnant of bourgeois law. That principle is in contradiction to the further development of the socialist forces. True it stimulates material engagement, but it does not contribute to the raising of a communist conscience."

I am here citing quotations of a somewhat earlier date, although since then there has been a certain retreat from such views. But this merely goes to confirm our argument, that communism cannot be created by subjectivistic political elaborations, but solely by the balanced evolution of all the material, ideological, cultural and political factors which constitute the basis of society.

We lack the data to enter into an exhaustive evaluation of the Chinese communes, that is, of their good and their bad aspects, nor do we wish to enter into those questions, which Chinese practice alone will decide. But one thing is certain, and that is that the Chinese communes of today in no respect whatsoever offer a form of socialist construc-

[1] An article of the Vice-President of the State Council, *Li Ksien Nien*, entitled *What I saw in the people's communes*, published in the *Peking Review* on November 11, 1958.

tion so attractive as to be likely to fill the working masses of other countries with enthusiasm for socialism.

The Chinese theoreticians clearly reduce the essence of communist distribution to payments in kind. In addition, they interpret Marx's idea that "an abundance of commodities" is necessary for communist distribution, as a requirement for the organs of state to decide how much anybody needs, whereas when he spoke of "an abundance of commodities" what Marx had in mind was a stage of highly developed productivity of labour in which the costs of production would be reduced to such a minimum that free distribution according to needs would be feasible, not state distribution. What is more, it is not that Marx preferred payments in kind to money payments; he merely presupposed that in a state of communism money would cease to exist, which, other things apart, would be because of this *free distribution according to needs*. Hence neither a system of payments in kind in itself, nor a directed levelling-out by state distribution can in any way contribute to the speedier development of communism. They are indeed even likely to slow that process down, if they begin to act as a brake on the development of the forces of production and of the productivity of labour, and here to talk about some sort of "socialist consciousness" in the abstract, separate from its material foundations and prime movers, is nothing but common and sterile idealistic lamentation.

Of course, as a very radical settling of accounts with all forms of private property relations in production, the Chinese people's communes, viewed through the prism of long-term development, may well play a very useful political role. But this is all dependent on the further development of the internal economic relation in them. In any case, in the form they assume today, the Chinese communes are a sort of "war communism" form and as such do not constitute a new phenomenon at all—even though they may be a step forward for China—nor can they be a stimulus to anybody else in the struggle for socialism. Such communes and any other such political and social relationships could only arise in a country with quite special conditions. First of all, China had just passed through a very long-lasting civil war and a war with an imperialist aggressor, in which wars the people had been reduced to extreme poverty and inured to bearing extreme deprivations in the interests of the victory of the revolution. In addition, China is characterized by small-scale agricultural production and poor rural semi-proletarians, who could serve as the political basis of a war communism *sui generis* based—at least ostensibly—on equality of poverty and of self-renunciation for the sake of a better morrow.

In a period of great revolutionary ideals and enthusiasm such sacrifices are not only possible and necessary, but do also in fact make it possible to take great steps forward in the mastering of the difficulties of an insufficiently developed economic basis. Our revolution too made this clear. Our people too for years deliberately underwent grave deprivations. But in course of time such renunciation turns into its opposite. Men renounce not only material goods, but also work, and this tendency on the one hand begins to destroy the productive forces by hampering the productivity of labour, and on the other—precisely through the efforts made to combat these tendencies—makes ever more extensive state interference in economic relations inevitable.

200

Consequently, such relationships cannot long be maintained. So long as their political basis is the small peasant and village semi-proletarian, this policy can probably yield certain results, but as the working-class strengthens, the contradictions based on those relationships will be exacerbated and will make the policy an untenable one. It is no accident that even today, despite formal decisions, the policy of "people's communes" is failing to work in the towns.

In a resolution of the Central Committee of the Communist Party of China the failure of the concept of the people's communes in the towns is explained in the following way:

"A bourgeois ideology still prevails among many capitalists and intellectuals in the towns. They still lack sufficient understanding of the formation of the communes, we shall have to wait a little for them to catch up. Consequently, we should persist in the carrying out of this experiment and, in general terms, should not be in a hurry to set up people's communes on a large scale in the towns.

Particularly in large towns this work should be postponed, except where necessary preparatory measures are required. The people's communes should be formed on a large scale in the towns only when we have acquired rich experience and the sceptics and doubters are convinced."[1]

However, it is not the ideology of the capitalists or intellectuals in question, but precisely the views of the working-class. The Chinese communes are the result of a specific synthesis of the leading influence of the state-ownership monopoly and of the primitive egalitarian aspirations of the rural semi-proletariat. For a certain time of

[1] *New China,* December 10, 1958.

basic revolutionary transformations such phenomena can even play a progressive part, particularly when one bears in mind that in present-day China five-sixths of the population live by agriculture and that the rural semi-proletariat and the small peasant were the main force of the revolution. However, the economic relationships which hold in the Chinese people's commune do not suit a developed working-class. For this reason, in China they will inevitably arouse ever greater resistance of the working-class which, as soon as it feels its own economic power, will not suffer any bureaucratic hegemony of formal equality, but will demand equality according to work done.

Li Ksien Nien, quoted above, clearly makes premature conclusions regarding "laziness" and "diligence".

Socialism can only win a victory over capitalism by a high level of productivity of labour. But higher productivity of labour than that of capitalism can only be given by a working-class which is developing and acting under conditions of free labour, that is, in the last resort, one which is liberated both from the domination of the private proprietor and from the pressure of any other social force apart from the individual and united producer.

This historic aim of the emancipation of labour, which certainly cannot be achieved overnight, can under the conditions of the transitional period and a relative insufficiency of consumer goods only be attained by the process of an ever more consistent development of social distribution based on the principle: to every man according to his labour. In the stage in which the given society is still unable to give everybody whatever his needs are, what suits not only economic needs, that is, the need for a material incentive to work, but also a healthy human sense of justice, is that people should receive in proportion to what they give the community. Any other way—if made a long-term policy—must inevitably lead not only to the undermining of the social-economic prerequisites of the struggle for higher productivity of labour, but also give rise to serious political consequences, to the appearance of political and even of antagonistic conflicts and in the last resort to grave deformations in social-economic relationships and in the system and policy of the socialist state.

Sooner or later, therefore, if they wish to overcome the tendency to stagnation in the development of the forces of production and of the productivity of labour the Chinese socialist forces too will have to pass to more developed forms of economic relations on the basis of the principle of distribution according to work done. Today, however, one still gets the impression that certain Chinese communists consider what is their virtue to be their weakness, and what is their weakness to be their virtue.

If that is how matters stand in China, it may be imagined what negative consequences would ensue if anybody tried to impose Chinese or any similar internal political and social-economic forms on any other country, particularly on one which was economically more developed, even though it be a capitalist country. It is clear that the imposing of such forms would result in a stagnation in the material foundations of the society, with a falling-off of productivity of labour and serious political conflicts.

However, it is not merely a matter here of social relationships such as those of the Chinese communes. In greater or less degree the same result would arise if anybody were to try, for instance, mechanically to transfer elsewhere the forms which arose in the October Revolution or in our own. Both the Russian and the Yugoslav revolutions took place in countries which were relatively backward economically, in countries of reactionary dictatorships, where every appearance of democratic ideas had been stifled. The automatic transfer of the experience and forms of those revolutions—even were we to presume them to be without faults, which is not the case—to any more developed country with a relatively firmly established democratic tradition, might result in a complete isolation of the revolutionary forces from the people.

In brief, socialism is not spread by simple repetition or extension of forms already achieved, but by the constant birth and perfection of new forms, which influence the old ones, enriching them and in this way stimulating them to the further advancement of socialism. *Anything that hinders this process, anything which is thrown into the process as an alien body—here meaning above all any form of political or ideological monopoly or domination—constitutes a brake, a temporary disturbance, the reflection of difficulties and deformations in the overcoming of the contradictions of the internal movements of socialist society, and for this reason needs to be submitted to the criticism of practice, which is possible only under conditions of the free development of the socialist relationships in every country separately.*

And here is why we Yugoslavs, in the name of socialism and as revolutionaries, are against the imposing of socialism or any particular socialist forms either by war or by any other form of force or pressure from without. We are convinced that socialism will exercise "pressure" by its

204

mere existence and this the more powerfully the more capable it is not only itself of renouncing force in international relations, but also of making it impossible for the forces of capitalism to resort to such force.

We have another instance in the relations between the socialist countries as the germs of future relations between the nations throughout the world. Were the Chinese theories to become the governing factor in socialist international policy, the relations between the socialist countries themselves would be doomed to fundamental deformation. Experience in the example of Yugoslavia shows that this has already happened once in history, and in no small way—in the period of the Stalinist pressure on Yugoslavia—and now it is the leadership of the Communist Party of China that is making another effort to introduce and "further develop" this policy of pressure on the internal socialist development of Yugoslavia and on Yugoslavia's international policy. For this attitude of theirs the Chinese theoreticians make little effort to find many reasons, theoretical or ideological.

Here is how they "explain" the essence of the policy of the Yugoslav communists:

"The League of Communists of Yugoslavia has declined to take part in the Moscow meeting of communist and working-class parties of the socialist countries or to sign the Declaration passed at that meeting. It stated that this was because the Moscow Declaration contained certain opinions and evaluations which were contrary to the attitude of the League of Communists of Yugoslavia, and which this considers wrong. For this act the Yugoslavs immediately received the recognition of the American imperialists...

On December 8th, 1957, Tito received the United States ambassador to Yugoslavia, James Riddleberger ... Immediately after this America granted a huge loan to Yugoslavia ... etc."[1]

Citing these words, I have no intention of going back to a discussion of the differences of opinion touching the Moscow Declaration. My only purpose is to point out how the Chinese theoreticians deal with important problems of socialist developments in our time which are the source of the differences of opinion between Yugoslavia and China.

The Chinese critics of our policy assert that Yugoslavia is a capitalist country, for the simple reason that we do not adopt those forms of internal socialist development which they adopt. Apart from this, they say that we are "imperialist agents" for the simple reason that we cannot agree with certain aspects of their international policy or their view of the relations between socialist countries. The differences of opinion on those matters serve the Chinese theoreticians to justify all their methods of pressure on socialist Yugoslavia.

At least since Marx we have known the characteristics which define the socialist character of a country. But the Chinese theoreticians have found a simpler formula: any country which is not formally in the organization known as the socialist camp is a capitalist country. Thereby Yugoslavia is automatically classed with the countries to which what anybody pleases may be done, all in the name of "socialism" and "Marxism". As the Chinese propagandists say, "a struggle to the very end should be waged against Yugoslav revisionism". What is the meaning of those words

[1] An article in *Jen min ji bao*, June 14, 1958, according to the *New China* agency.

"to the very end"? It can mean nothing else but that a socialist country which does not endorse Chinese views and demands can be settled with by force. This certainly throws a light "to the very end" on the Chinese theory of what constitutes just and what unjust war.

A wonderful logic indeed, one certainly worthy of "true Marxists". Such logic means that a country is a socialist country if it accepts the Chinese views in entirety, while if it does not, it remains a capitalist country, even though its social-economic relationships are socialist.

It goes without saying that I have not spent all this time on this particular Chinese attitude to Yugoslav socialism because we have any particular desire to have anybody "recognize" our socialism. I have however thought it necessary in plain words to point to this factor because it is symptomatic of the Chinese concepts of the relations between socialist countries. Anybody can see where this sort of unprincipled and narrow pragmatic "Marxism", more like the right of the stronger than any kind of ideology, could lead the relations between the socialist countries, and to what extent it is capable of distorting them.

For that matter, it may very easily happen that the Chinese theoreticians find themselves without this theory of theirs which classes Yugoslavia in the capitalist camp, for now a really strange contradiction develops. Yugoslavia, which is not in the socialist camp, supports the basic concepts of the international policy of that camp concerning peaceful coexistence and peace. But China, which is in the camp, criticizes this policy. How do these Chinese conceptions of the camp and the validity of the line of argument about the capitalist nature of Yugoslavia now stand?

Here we see to what troublesome situations the narrow pragmatic habit of cloaking very clear policies with very hazy theories can lead theoreticians.

Mao Tse-tung once wrote the following:

"Those who counsel us to apply the experience of the Soviet Union in unchanged form, taking no account of the specific features of our situation, are in fact suggesting that we should shorten our feet to make them fit the short shoes of Soviet theory and practice . . .

The consequence of the action of those dogmaticians was that we lost all the foundations of the revolution."

It looks as if today, forcing certain conceptions of theirs on ourselves and others, the Chinese leaders forget these words of Mao Tse-tung's, or think they apply only to them, and not to others. Today they would like to force those tiny shoes on us and they are angry because we refuse to accept them.

Apart from this, it seems that the Chinese critics of Yugoslavia have also forgotten the following words of the well-known Declaration which their government made on November 1, 1956:

"Because of these errors in the relations between the socialist countries, some of those countries were unable to build a form of socialism which would better fit their historical circumstances and special conditions . . . To maintain unity of ideology and the aims of the struggle, it often happens that certain personalities of the socialist countries infringe the principle of equality between the nations in their mutual relations. In its nature such an error is an error of bourgeois chauvinism. Such an error, particularly that which consists in the chauvinism of a great country, inevitably leads to the infliction of serious harm on the solidarity and the common cause of the socialist countries."

Is it not precisely into this "error" that certain present-day leaders of Chinese policy are falling?

They are free to disagree with us. They are free to shed all responsibility for our acts and our policy, that is, free not to support it when they do not agree with it. They are even free to criticize us. But there are two things which they must do if they wish to remain Marxists and revolutionaries: first, they must take account of the fact that despite all differences of opinion Yugoslavia is a socialist country, and secondly, it is their duty with all seriousness to analyse the essence of those differences of opinion. If they do not do this, it certainly is not because they are insufficiently acquainted with Marxism, but because they have different views on the relations between socialist countries, and that fact merely goes still more to confirm the correctness of our criticism of the Chinese theories of this sort.

By this attitude, Chinese policy openly and crudely disrupts the unity of the socialist world. Instead of seeking those elements which tend to unite the socialist countries on a basis of equality, it emphasizes differences in order, criticizing them, to impose its own political monopoly. In the name of what? Clearly, not in the name of socialism, for socialism and domination of others certainly do not go together.

Consequently, not only because of those political consequences in the capitalist countries which are detrimental to the cause of socialism, and not only because of the danger of catastrophic destruction which an eventual world war would inevitably entail, but before all else for the sake of the healthy development of socialism in the world and for the sake of the development of relations between the socialist countries themselves, it is indispensable to abandon this pseudo-leftist criticism of the policy of coexistence, and also the course of policy based on the inevitability of war.

CHAPTER 14

Causes and Consequences

As we emphasized at the outset, the Chinese policy is not merely a consequence of "a deviation from the line of Marxism", nor an accident, but is the natural, political result of the structure and contradictions of the world today. For this reason it will tend to appear for some considerable period of time, in this form or that, with varying degrees of intensity, as a trend of international political relationships in our time, till the conditions which create it change, at least to a certain degree. As those conditions are not immutable or insuperable, the hope is justified that sooner or later Chinese socialism will indeed overcome its present oscillations.

The peoples of China, whom imperialist pressure and the internal feudal *régimes* kept under fierce exploitation and in prolonged backwardness, found their own way out of their internal contradictions in revolution and the prospects of socialism. The Chinese Revolution has been one of the greatest revolutionary epics in the history of mankind. But the revolutionary war which in China lasted all but twenty-five years, against the united forces of China's own reactionaries and of international imperialism, does not merely bear witness to its profundity or the sharpness of the contradictions which made that revolution indispensable, but also of the great responsibilities of that revolution to its own people. One of the main factors which had made the revolution indispensable, namely, the relative economic backwardness of the country, has however now become the main obstacle to any speed in internal development, and the principal source of the danger of internal reactionary forces rising again and undermining the unity of the country. The settlement of this issue now brings into question the very survival of the revolution. The people which has shed so much blood in the long drawn-out revolution now with justice expects that victorious revolution to open up new prospects in just this sphere.

In a Report on the work of the Government made in May, 1957, Liu Shao Chi declared that the "speed of building up the country constitutes the most important question of all those with which we have had to contend since the victory of the socialist revolution".

In these words we have the clearest expression of the essence of the principal internal contradiction in the development of Chinese society.

The struggle against those problems is an exceptionally hard one. China has received and is still receiving a certain amount of economic aid from the socialist countries. But however great that aid, and no matter in what it consists, it cannot be sufficient to ensure the speeded-up economic expansion of a country which is a continent in itself. For the economic development of China to be normal, it needs to be an integral part of world economy.

On the other hand, China has been constantly exposed to the persistent pressure of the capitalist world, in particular of the United States of America, which vainly hopes that this will weaken the revolution and strengthen the counter-revolutionary forces. When open intervention proved unfeasible, an economic blockade of China was organized and efforts were made to secure the country's complete political isolation. The door to the United Nations and to other organizations of international cooperation was closed. Apart from this, a constant threat is levelled against China by the artificial maintenance of the counter-revolutionary *régime* on Formosa and the establishment of military bases all round China. As a result, not only is it made impossible for China to find a place in world trade which would contribute to a more normal internal economic development, and not only does China receive no support whatsoever from world economy, but pressure is additionally exerted to increase the country's material burdens.

All these facts have very greatly increased the strains to which the peoples of China are subjected in their efforts to overcome backwardness and build up new social relationships, and that increase in the necessary effort has had as a consequence an increased sense that only self-reliance and extreme sacrifices on the part of the Chinese peoples and forces themselves can give any results. It was all the easier for such a feeling to arise since we have here a huge country, with hundreds of millions of inhabitants. It is perfectly natural under such conditions that there should have arisen a tendency to feel that the encircling ring imposed on China by the capitalist states by pressure and force must be broken by counter pressure and—if necessary—by force. Under such circumstances, to many Chinese, unable to take an integral view of social developments in the whole world, a policy based on coexistence not only looks unlike practical politics, but is even felt to be likely to contribute to the maintenance of this state in which the peoples of

China are now situated, that is, they see it as a brake on Chinese progress.

In its essence this sort of resistance to pressure from outside is not only understandable but also completely justifiable throughout. It should be clear to anyone that such a great country as China cannot long be kept blockaded and isolated, without such a situation giving rise to consequences serious for the whole world. The vital forces which indubitably exist cannot be stifled. Pressure merely results in their finding some other, often enough a purely elemental way out. This is the more so since China's efforts to overcome backwardness and against the external pressure of the imperialist forces which till yesterday ruled in Asia, and in that continent have left behind them nothing but poverty and backwardness, correspond to the elementary interests of the great part of mankind of today in Asia and in the other continents. Not only are many peoples here forced to live in that backwardness and poverty, but there is also no way out for them, no practical, satisfactory prospect likely in the foreseeable future to liberate them from one and the other condition. What I have in mind is the part played by the problem of the insufficiently developed countries, a problem which is becoming an ever more acute and large-scale international problem. This problem is still further exacerbated by the fact that now, after the collapse of colonial and similar forms of political subordination, the forces of imperialism are trying to secure their political hegemony by means of a pressure which exploits the economic backwardness of certain countries. These problems in one country and another give rise to the most varied trends and political activities, all boiling down to a demand for a definite share-out of resources among all the nations of the world in one or another form. Such demands may suit or not suit some people, but they are a fact, born of the material contradiction by which the world of today is divided into developed and insufficiently developed countries. In the last resort, if even a great part of the working-class—not to speak of the bourgeoisie, and here and there even the majority of the working-class—fails to show sufficient understanding of the position of the economically backward nations or the problem of how to overcome their poverty, can we reasonably expect the workers and peasants of an economically backward a land as China to understand the views of the "rich" nations?

In itself, of course, this question is not a problem of the struggle for socialism, but in the complex of world contradictions it is connected with that struggle. Taken by itself, it is a problem not only for the world as a whole, but also one which appears within the socialist countries. In this aspect for a long time to come it will constitute one of the very important material and also political contradictions in the development of socialism. At the same time, the distinction lies in the fact that within a socialist economy this problem can be tackled more easily and more quickly by the conscious action of the socialist forces, by overcoming the effect of egoism in one and another direction, so that it is dealt with by material evolution itself. On the other hand, however, in the world of today, in which precisely in the most developed countries we have capitalist relationships, which inevitably breed imperialistic economic and political expansion wherever this can hold its ground, there is a tendency for the gulf between the developed and the underdeveloped countries to become even more profound. Here too is the source of the essential resistance of the forces of reaction to the system of organized international aid to the undeveloped countries, even to any form of economic aid, except in so far as "aid" is taken to mean the export of capital under the customary conditions of the capitalist world. The capitalist countries depart from this practice only when compelled to do so by political realities, which are sometimes—and, in the new relations of the social forces of the world, more often too—more powerful than their immediate economic interests.

It is thus natural for the peoples of Asia and Africa to see in their struggle against backwardness and economic exploitation by foreign capital a continuation of their struggle for national independence. Similarly, it is inevitable for that struggle to be linked with the struggle against colonialism and imperialism, and with the struggle for socialism.

Consequently, those reactionary circles which think that all these problems can be kept "on ice" by the policy of pressure on China, by the policy of economic blockade and political isolation of China, fail to realize that they are sowing a wind, but will reap a hurricane. In Asia and Africa the calm is already disappearing and the storm beginning. Developments which show how untenable are various western-democratic models of political systems in those countries are the most convincing symptom of the fact.

Now, the Chinese concepts of an international policy for socialism are also a form of direct reaction to the same problems, but one which from the standpoint of socialism is out of shape. When I say that we have here a reaction which from the standpoint of socialism is out of shape, what I have in mind is the fact that in those concepts the problem of Asia and Africa and altogether of the countries which are breaking free or striving to break free from backwardness and alien economic domination is not treated as one of the problems and sources of the revolutionary struggle for socialism, but on the contrary, all the historic interests of socialism are in this sphere subordinated to the specific state interests and aims of China, that is, to the interests formed under such conditions. In other words, China wants to impose herself on others as a political force not for the defence of peace and socialism but to overcome her own difficulties and to attain her own material aims. It goes without saying that were such a tendency to prevail, material and political conditions would thereby be created in which not only would the development of socialism be subjected to grave deformations, but the most reactionary circles in the world would even *regain strength* as defenders of the principle of national independence. Consequently, a policy based on such tendencies is likely to bring serious defeats not only upon China but also the whole of international socialism.

Nevertheless, while criticizing the unsocialist and detrimental ways in which Chinese policy reacts to China's complex of internal problems, which we have discussed above, not for one iota do we diminish the responsibility of those Western countries which have to a great extent contributed to the creation in China of the conditions for the formation of such a line of policy. Of course, the internal development of China cannot be exclusively ascribed to the policy of the U.S.A. and other Western countries, but there can be no doubt whatsoever that this factor bears the greater part of the responsibility for present relations.

Therefore what is required is to strive for the curtailment of the political blockade, of discrimination against China, of the political and economic isolation of China. We need stubbornly to work to ensure that the atmosphere of relaxation in the world, which has already produced good results, should be further consolidated by agreements in the sphere of disarmament and collective security. We should continue and increase the vigour of the fight for an organized international action of aid for the speedier economic development of the insufficiently developed countries. We should further give support to the struggle of the nations to break free not only from political but also from economic dependence. The fight for these and other such democratic principles and demands in international relations is one of the basic methods by which support may be given by the international forces of socialism to all peoples in the liberation struggle and to all the forces of progress.

Of course, so long as mankind is not able to overcome the resistance of the vestiges of colonialism, imperialism and every sort of hegemony, it would be unpractical to expect that democratic relations between the peoples could be ensured or that it is feasible to create a really efficacious and satisfactory international mechanism of economic aid. The final solution of that problem lies solely in the economic and political unification of the world through internal social processes and forces acting in all parts of the world, which in the last resort is only realizable when socialist relations dominate also in the economic relations between the nations. But that does not mean that we should wait with folded arms till this has come about. The very struggle to make today's international relations more progressive and to provide economic aid for the undeveloped countries is in fact precisely one of the factors of development in that direction. Further, practice has shown that certain results can be attained even today and that they can gradually be extended, parallel to internal social progress, in one country and another, and together with the consolidation of the policy of coexistence. In any case, the socialist countries cannot solve those problems by war, for that method of tackling them would bring the socialist countries into conflict not only with the bourgeoisie but also with the working-class of other countries.

I can readily advance the argument that the Chinese critics of Yugoslav policy will advance, that here again I am "putting a fine face on" imperialism, ascribing to it a capability of adopting democratic relationships between nations and of aid to the undeveloped countries, even the socialist ones among them. But here I am not discussing imperialism and its qualities, which not only Marxists but also all democratically-minded men in the world know quite well, I am discussing the set-up of the world today, and this is no longer under the absolute domination of imperialism.

Imperialism still plays a significant part in the world, but this also contains the growing force of socialism. There is the anti-imperialist outlook of the nations liberated from colonialism, which do not need to pass through all the phases of capitalist development to get to socialism, and there are also other powerful socialist and progressive forces outside the framework of the communist parties, which are beginning to grasp the indispensability of social changes in the world of capitalism, and also in international relations. It is obvious that all these progressive forces taken as a whole, will both as political and as material factors be increasingly capable, in the climate of the policy of coexistence, of forcing back reactionary tendencies and winning through to the victory of socialist principles in one sector and another of international relations, to the extent to which that force of socialism grows. It goes without saying that the decisive factor in such a process is the stubborn struggle of the socialist and anti-imperialist forces in every country, using the means which correspond to the particular time and particular conditions of each country.

One of the factors which have influenced the Chinese course based on the inevitability of war is the state of the international workers' movement.

It is undeniable that the working-class of the Western countries has not given sufficiently effective support to the justified efforts of the Chinese people to end the world-wide policy of pressure, blockade and isolation, organized against China. What is more, among the supporters of that policy have even been many social-democratic circles, blinded by their short-sighted anti-communism. Nor has the American working-class taken any serious step to make it clear that it does not support the official policy in this respect. Why, even in the countries in which they are strong even the communist parties have not shown themselves capable of giving the working-class any effective lead into an active fight against the anti-Chinese policy.

There is no question about it, this has been one of the factors which in China have hardened the conviction not only that that country must rely exclusively on its own strength, but also that the victory of socialism in the West is feasible in no other way, but only through a world war.

Of course, all this provides an explanation of the causes of the Chinese views, but it does not justify those views. The state of affairs in the working-class of the Western countries which I have described above did not come into being all by itself, accidentally. It too has its sources and causes. Some of these are connected with the internal social-economic order of those countries and the structure of the working-class itself, while others are connected with the internal and external subjective factors which influence the particular working-class. Among those factors—not to speak here of others—is this Chinese policy itself. One could hardly describe it as a policy calculated to win the hearts of the workers of those countries. On the contrary, it has frequently repelled them. This policy has frightened the workers more often than it has the bourgeoisie, and one of the ways it has done this has been such an incomprehensible action as the anti-Yugoslav campaign. For this reason present-day Chinese policy has never acted as an influence making for a different stand on the part of the working-class, but on the contrary has worked towards making the working-class assume a passive attitude, and on occasion has even served to unite a larger or smaller portion of the workers with the bourgeoisie on the same platform, with a more or less united foreign policy. In addition, inside the social-democratic parties this Chinese policy has strengthened those circles whose "socialist" programme consists exclusively of anti-communism.

In reality, there is no reason to believe that the working-class of the Western countries would be in favour of a blockade of China or of a war against China, but on the other hand there is no socialist ideal which could be held to justify forcing socialism from outside, by war, on a working-class under the influence of reformism. On the contrary, all reasons speak in favour of a socialist policy such that would fundamentally convince the workers of any non-socialist country or any ideology whatsoever that the socialist countries will never force either socialism or their will on anybody by war or any pressure at all from outside. Only under such conditions will the working-class —regardless of its party adherence—really act like a working-class, that is, turn its attention to the problems of internal social developments and be an active support of the forces of peace and it will then be harder for the forces of reaction to deceive the working-class as to the real substance of their international political acts.

However, instead of the authors of Chinese international policy drawing the conclusion from all this that they should direct their policy towards establishing links with a working-class likely to react in that way concerning current common interests, that is, the questions of peace, coexistence and democratic relations between the nations; what they have done is to still further exacerbate the sectarian trend of their policy. Their setting a course based on the inevitability of war and a frontal clash between "the eastern and the western wind", together with a whole series of actions, one of which is this anti-Yugoslav campaign, tends to give rise to a lack of confidence, not to say even fear in the ranks of the working-class of other countries. It is quite patent that thereby China is in no way making it easier for herself to tackle a number of burning problems.

At the same time the leading circles in China have adopted the course of an all-out mobilization of their internal forces, even at the cost of the greatest hardships for the people. This mobilization is so all-embracing and so intensive that it has made the whole system of internal ecomonic and political relations subordinate to it. In certain fields this mobilization has undoubtedly given significant material results. But as one of the phases of development of the revolution it is on the point of exhausting itself. Not only that that historic effort which in itself is progressive, nevertheless, as it begins in a certain sense to become an end in itself—since dogmatic and conservative thought imposes it as a permanent essence of socialism—and because it begins to become a brake on the advance of socialist economic relations precisely in the most advanced sector of production—gives rise to the germ of a new contradiction, which in course of time cannot but begin to undermine precisely that great revolutionary effort. Here I have in mind the contradiction between the centralized administrative management of production and distribution on the one hand, which unquestionably gives rise to a conservative bureaucratism and a trend to the petrification of state hired-labour relations, and on the other hand the demand of the workers for distribution according to work done, which inevitably gives rise to a need for an appropriate system of industrial management such that will liberate labour from the pressure of state hired-labour relations.

Of course, this process requires a rather long evolution. We would be sterile idealists and abstract dream-spinners indeed, were we to expect or want to see this contradiction decided overnight by a subjective decision of the Chinese leadership. However, the problem is not that of a "final" solution, but whether the conditions exist for an unhindered evolution towards one. Today paths of such an evolution in China are by reason of the policy under discussion closed or at least seriously encumbered, therefore the contradictions cannot but grow worse and tend to produce certain distortions both in economic and political life. Under such conditions one of the first reactions is unquestionably a weakening of personal incentives to greater productivity of labour, which calls for an increased application of administrative supervision and thereby leads straight to all sorts of bureaucratic distortions of socialist development. Such a situation gives rise to a powerful political monopoly of the centre, while, further, with lack of economic strength and under the influence of internal contradictions such a centre, based on strong political authority, may well fall a victim to the illusion that by its political power alone it can tackle and solve problems which in reality can only be settled by material evolution.

Since such efforts are unpractical, every further step of material advancement finds expression in an increase in the material efforts and sacrifices of the people. To justify such sacrifices, or in other words, to keep the mass of the people mobilized for those sacrifices, the Chinese theoreticians have without any need or advantage invented a whole ideology. Humanism has been declared to be petty-bourgeois hypocrisy. The aspiration for "personal happiness" has been condemned as anti-socialist individualism. Democratic tendencies have been represented as ridiculous Philistine prejudices. Criticism of bureaucratic-*étaliste* monopolism has been attacked as revisionism of the worst kind.

It goes without saying that ideological tendencies of this sort could not but come to further expression in Chinese international policy. Such great sacrifices can certainly only be called for and justified if it is a matter not only of a programme for a brighter future but also one of national independence and a definite position for the Chinese nation in international relations, one to which China has a right, but which the United States of America and other capitalist countries dispute. Hence the policy of the cold war and of frightening people by threat of war not only does not hinder these Chinese efforts on the home front, but even makes them easier to bear.

Here unquestionably we have some of the main sources and causes of the Chinese criticism of the policy of coexistence and of their adopting the policy of cold war. Of course there are others too, but in the framework of the subjects of this examination there is no need for me to enter into an analysis of factors which have no direct connection with them.

However, under present-day conditions to adopt the cold war policy does not only mean "frightening", "bringing pressure to bear" and so on, it also means directly strengthening, even creating and organizing the forces of war in the capitalist countries; in other words, like it or not, it means preparing war. Herein precisely lies the danger of the present Chinese policy.

o

Socialism and War

From the standpoint of any "tactical aims" or methods whatsoever it is senseless to talk of peace and coexistence, yet threaten war. The struggle for peace has its own language and its own means, but neither threats of war nor pressure on others, neither menacing others nor the cold war are among them. Whoever wants to seem convincing in the struggle for peace and coexistence should first and foremost struggle against such phenomena and methods.

In the West there are circles which are for a policy called "neither war nor peace". It would seem that the authors of some Chinese press articles support a similar international policy. But both these and those are very myopic politicians. Even at the time of October Revolution these "tactics", which Trotsky and others supported, proved untenable, and Lenin decisively rejected them. But above all today, when opposed one to the other we have two huge concentrations of weapons of war, every sober-minded man should know that tactics of "neither war nor peace" do not mean anything else but—preparation for war, even instigation of war.

Precisely for this reason there is no real distinction at all between the threat or menace of war and the preparation and instigation of war.

Of course, *it is one thing to draw up one's aims and demands properly, and another to discover effective means and weapons for the realization of those aims which are appropriate to the given conditions of struggle.* It is here that we have the contradictoriness of the Chinese policy, and not only the Chinese foreign policy but also a considerable field of their home policy. Examining their own problems within their national frontiers which, extensive as they are, from the standpoint of socialism as a world system are still cramped, and lacking sufficient confidence in the strength of world socialism, precisely because these internal forces of Chinese socialism are weak, the Chinese political leaders have decided on a policy which not only is not capable of solving the problems which it was invented to solve, but one which on the contrary will merely go to increase the difficulties which the Chinese Revolution has to overcome. And not only have they come out against the policy of coexistence, which would have been the quickest path to breaking the blockade which encloses China, but the leading circles of China have also decided on all sorts of international acts which have excited the unanimous resistance precisely of those peoples who were the closest and most natural allies of China in the struggle for the final liberation of Asia from the vestiges of imperialist rule and for the overcoming of the backwardness of the Asian peoples. This policy has gone so far that that great country has even begun to stir up outstanding, but very trifling frontier problems, which certainly is not at all in harmony with the spirit of a socialist foreign policy. In this way, instead of confidence, the Chinese policy is creating fear all round its frontiers, and fear gives new strength to the policy of the blockade, just when this had begun to be discredited and markedly weakened.

What is more, by her insistence on subordinating the interests and views of world socialism to her own interests and views, China has come into conflict with the socialist forces as well. It is completely clear that such a policy cannot make it any easier for China to resolve her own internal problems, but even more is it clear that it is doing serious harm to the further expansion of socialism in the world.

Such a foreign policy will undoubtedly have its repercussions also on the internal development of China, in the sense of a further political and economic centralization, an extreme strengthening of the apparatus of the state and the control by this of the whole of internal life. And such phenomena will be not merely an inexhaustible source of bureaucratic-*étatiste* distortions of socialist development —that is, of conservative yearnings to preserve and bolster up state-capitalist forms in social relationships—but also a cause of new economic difficulties, and first and foremost of a still slower growth of productivity of labour and of a still lower profitability of investments. Such development will impose on the people still greater sacrifices and will still further exacerbate the contradictions of material developments. This is in fact a spiral which inevitably leads the whole conception up a blind alley.

Social development has its own insuperable laws, which will not yield to any man's wishful thinking, not even that of the Chinese. Everybody who has tried ignoring those laws, by following a course of subjective elaborations of policy, instead of remaining on the solid ground of a real analysis of the actual conditions, has suffered defeat. Nor will the Chinese communists be able sooner or later to avoid feeling the consequences of their policy of scorning the objective laws governing things. We can only hope that those failures, which even now have begun to draw the attention of the communists of China to the dangers facing them, will, in Lenin's words, be that factor which in the end will persuade them to abandon a sterile political course which cannot give a lasting solution to any one of their problems.

CHAPTER 15

The Chinese-Yugoslav Differences of Opinion

History itself creates the cure for every ailment. The phenomena of contradictions which have so clearly come to expression in the development of the socialist world, and which perhaps trouble and frighten some short-sighted people, will at the same time help those who fight for socialism better to understand the problems of present-day socialism and not be contented with interpreting this or that phenomenon in the course of development by the simple repetition of stereotyped dogmatic phrases.

This also applies to the Chinese-Yugoslav differences of opinion. Today it must be clear to every Marxist that these differences of opinion are not the fruit of any abstract ideological-theoretical disputes about the interpretation of Marxism, nor are they the fruit of any sort of Yugoslav "national communism", nor of any Yugoslav infringement of the principles of socialist internationalism or so forth, as has so often been maintained in the attacks on the communists of Yugoslavia, *but are in their essence the reflection of real contradictions of socialist development which arise from the fact that in its forms, its paths and its means socialism is not a process which is repeated every time and everywhere in the same way, but is one which never appears anywhere in a "pure" form, that is, free from all the influences of the material and ideological elements of the given period, environment and conditions.*

229

Under such conditions the right of the people freely to decide on the ways and means of socialist development is a principle which guarantees not only equality among the peoples but, still more important, also the most rapid and painless development and advance of world socialism. Precisely for this reason we have always fought for that principle, and today still fight, in regard to the Chinese anti-Yugoslav campaign.

This also applies to the principle of socialist solidarity. That principle too finds expression in varied ways, in varied acts and organizations, but what is essential is that it unites the socialist forces on basic questions of the defence and consolidation of the socialist achievements. The essence of this principle is not any formal unity nor is it in any mechanical discipline, but in a real and profound sense of the identity of the elementary interests of the socialist forces in all quarters of the world. But this sense is possible only on the basis of the complete equality of rights and of self-government of all the peoples on the socialist road.

In his time Engels wrote:

"The international movement of the European and American proletariat has become so much strengthened that not merely its first narrow form—the secret League— but even its second infinitely wider form—the open International Workingmen's Association—has become a fetter for it, so that the feeling of solidarity based on the understanding of the identity of class position is sufficient to create and to hold together one and the same great party of the proletariat among the workers of all countries and tongues."[1]

[1] Marx-Engels: *Selected Works*, International Publishers, New York, Vol. II, pp. 26—27.

What then is to be said about the present-day strength of the international working-class movement? Are we to consider that the awareness of the identity of the basic class interests of the socialist forces is less developed today than it once was? It is clear that we should not look at things in that way, for that would be to negate not only the experience of our time but also the very teachings of Marxism about the class struggle. However, for precisely this awareness to be the real basis of socialist solidarity, the principle of solidarity should never be set in opposition to the principle of the independent determination and testing in practice of the varied forms and ways of socialist development, including here the international policy of socialism. In other words, the concrete forms of solidarity should not blot out the possibility of a democratic clearing up of the problems of socialist advancement by testing them through varied implementations and through democratic forms of the struggle of ideas.

For these reasons we Yugoslav communists have never avoided open discussion between the communists of the various countries about the problems of present-day realities and the advancement of socialism. In fact, we have considered it useful and indispensable, of course on condition that it does not destroy the sense of mutual responsibility in matters concerning the solidarity of the progressive forces. This also holds as regards the difference between our views and the Chinese conceptions of a socialist international policy. If the Chinese communists really wished in principle to clear up any of the problems of present-day prospects of the further development of socialism, and if such discussion were kept within the limits and forms of discussion appro-

231

priate between equal partners, this might be advantageous, even were it impossible to make both sides' views fit each other. In the last resort, we have never held that the aim of discussions of this sort is the removal of all differences of opinion, for today that is becoming an impossibility, when communists are no longer merely a revolutionary movement struggling for power, but are at the head of a number of states and are becoming the expression of the most varied material developments. Differences of opinion as to various questions of tactics, methods of struggle and how to approach the resolution of this or that problem cannot fail to exist under present-day conditions. The point, however, of such discussions, is precisely that despite differences of opinion they tend to ensure that indispensable solidarity of the socialist and the progressive forces which strengthens socialism and the progress of mankind as a whole and is their defence against reactionary attacks.

To attain this sort of discussion between communists, the methods introduced by Stalin, who pronounced anybody who had his own opinion about socialist policy to be some sort of traitor to socialism, must be rejected. In other words, now that at last the cult of personality and the political methods which arose from that cult have been condemned, discussion between communists should also be freed from the methods of slander, interruption, lies, distortions, insinuations, the attachment of all manner of ideological labels, and this precisely in order, quite apart from the differences of opinion, to ensure socialist solidarity also regarding questions of common interests, on the basis of complete equality.

232

In this framework what is both feasible and necessary is also mutual criticism conducted in a democratic way. The Yugoslav communists do not consider themselves proof against error, or infallible, but they cannot admit anybody else, whoever it may be, to have a monopoly right to the determination of the truth or the paths of socialist practice either in internal or external politics. For this reason criticism is an indispensable instrument for the clearing up of points of dispute. But as Lenin has already said, criticism can take two forms, which are always dependent on the purpose of the criticism, one is the method of criticism which aims at destroying, the other the method of criticism which desires to assist. Among communists and all socialist and progressive forces, even when very profound differences of opinion exist over matters of principle, the methods of constructive criticism should prevail. And such criticism also has its own language, methods and democratic forms.

In contradistinction to the Chinese anti-Yugoslav propaganda, and despite insults, we have always striven in our criticism of Chinese policy to remain on the level of this latter kind of criticism. This we intend to go on doing. We have no desire to impose our views on the Chinese communists, not merely because we have neither the will to do so nor the possibility of doing so, but also because such acts would be most profoundly counter to those democratic principles for which we stand and on which the mutual relations of the peoples and of the movements in the world of socialism should be built and developed. Differences of opinion which cannot be brushed aside should be settled by evolution and by experience, not by antagonistic exacerbation of ill feeling.

But, it goes without saying, we also cannot allow anybody to force their views on us by pressure, political or otherwise. Mutual criticism is one thing, but the introduction of force into mutual relations is another. And any political pressure —outside the framework of a democratic criticism—in the framework of the relations between the socialist countries we consider to be a hegemonistic exercise of force. This is precisely why we also cannot accept the line of argument of the Chinese critics of Yugoslavia according to which it is the duty of the Yugoslav communists to stand in line with Chinese socialism, though the Chinese communists have no similar obligation to Yugoslav socialism.

The current Chinese anti-Yugoslav campaign has taken over the thoroughly discredited legacy of the Stalin campaign of 1948 and subsequent years. Clearly here we have not to do with the criticism or the discussion of which I spoke above, but with an act of political pressure, one which is precisely aimed at silencing such criticism and discussion. Thus savagely attacking the Yugoslav communists, the Chinese leaders obviously would like to create an atmosphere in which anybody who does not mechanically repeat the ultra-radical and sectarian phrases of the Chinese lexicon would thereby automatically declare himself to be an adherent of "Yugoslav revisionism". And this of itself is a proof that we have to do here not with socialist solidarity but with a struggle for an ideological and political monopoly, for the realization of certain fixed notions about the international and internal policy of socialism.

Of course, once we are confronted by such trends and such methods of pressure on a socialist country, we cannot remain silent. We cannot permit the Chinese propagandists

234

to besmirch and slander socialist Yugoslavia without giving them an auswer, the less so because by so doing they are undermining the most progressive aspirations of present-day socialism as a whole, of which unquestionably one of the most revolutionary, most progressive and most noble is precisely the struggle for peace and for peaceful coexistence.

Perhaps in some countries men will be found who will condemn our answering the Chinese protagonists of the anti-Yugoslav campaign back, considering this detrimental to the general interests of socialism. Perhaps such people think that silence would be more profitable. But socialist Yugoslavia also has her own interests and she cannot allow anybody in the name of a false "socialism" to trample on those interests in the most crude manner. But that is not the most important thing. It would be more harmful than any public argument to allow anybody to fish in muddied waters, that is, in conditions where the working masses do not really know what it is all about. The Yugoslav communists are under an obligation to tell their own people—and not only their own people, but also the international proletariat as a whole, what the essence of the Chinese-Yugoslav differences of opinion really is.

And finally, to assume an attitude regarding the tackling of the large and decisive problems of present-day socialism is certainly an unavoidable historical task of today's generation of revolutionary socialists, and for this reason we Yugoslav communists are firmly covinnced that frank replies to these Chinese attacks, equally openly pronounced and published, can only be of advantage to the cause of socialism, for they will bring more clarity into the problems under discussion.

The forces of reaction, let me add, hope in vain to extract some advantage for themselves from this. Everything that leads to the consolidation of a line of policy based on coexistence will also build up the confidence of the people in the possibility of maintaining lasting peace, it will increase the number and the strength of the adherents of coexistence in the capitalist world as well, and this not only inside the working-class and the anti-imperialist movements in that world, but also in other sober circles of society which do not want mankind to be exposed to the catastrophe of a new world war, that is, those who are beginning to grasp that what is historically unavoidable in the development of society cannot be escaped.

In conclusion, it is necessary once again to emphasize that it would be very mistaken to look at the totality of the role and development of the Chinese revolution through the prism of the differences of opinion under discussion here. We must not forget the epoch-making past which the Chinese Revolution has played in our age. It is this revolution which dealt the system of imperialism and colonialism in Asia and in the other continents a fatal blow, thereby playing a decisive part in radically changing the whole relationship of forces in the present-day world. The men who under the most arduous conditions led that revolution and by their abilities proved one of the significant factors in its victory are today still largely at the head of China. Consequently, whatever the transitory distortions in Chinese policy, we are sure that Chinese socialism will master them. But precisely for this reason it is so much the more necessary to criticize these phenomena openly, and this the more so since it is they that are the source of the Chinese anti-Yugoslav campaign.

Throughout its development the Yugoslav communists gave the Chinese Revolution active political support. And when the revolutionary Government of the new China was installed, Yugoslavia was one of the first to recognize it and give it her support, both in the United Nations and outside it. At that time, carrying out Stalin's anti-Yugoslav line, the Chinese Government did not consider it necessary even to reply to the Yugoslav proposals for the establishment of normal relations between the two countries. But this nevertheless in no way changed the attitude of approval of revolutionary China which Yugoslavia had adopted, nor did it weaken Yugoslav support of the justified Chinese demands in international politics.

This is how today we still look on new China and our relations with her. We wish the Chinese peoples may see their efforts to build the material basis for socialism crowned with the greatest success. In addition, we desire Chinese-Yugoslav relations to be based on the principle of mutual aid one to the other in the building of socialism, without imposing any ready-made ideological or political schemes one on the other. In that spirit we shall continue further stubbornly doing all that lies in our power to secure an improvement of our relations with China and the Chinese communists, for in our view it is solely on such a basis that cooperation between two socialist countries can develop with success.

But this does not depend on us alone. If the price of such cooperation has to be renunciation of the principles of our independent socialist domestic and foreign policies—

independent not of the interests of socialism but of any other people's particular subjectively concocted notions—in this case those of the Communist Party of China—it must be said outright that this is a price we are not prepared to pay, for it would mean the renunciation under pressure from without of precisely those basic and most essential principles which should govern the relations between socialist countries.